A TRAVELER'S GUIDE TO 116

Michigan Lighthouses

Text: Laurie Penrose

Maps: Bill T. Penrose

Black and White Photos: Ruth Penrose

Color Photos: Bill J. Penrose

Friede Publications

Friede Publications
2339 Venezia Drive
Davison, Michigan 48423
514 Waukazoo Avenue
Petoskey, Michigan 49770

Printed in the United States of America

First printing, April 1992
Second printing, June 1993
Third printing, November 1994
Fourth Printing, July 1996
Fifth Printing, March 1999
Sixth Printing, July 2001

ISBN 0-923756-03-5

OTHER GUIDEBOOKS BY FRIEDE PUBLICATIONS

A Traveler's Guide to 100 Eastern Great Lakes Lighthouses

A Traveler's Guide to 116 Western Great Lakes Lighthouses

A Guide to 199 Michigan Waterfalls

Natural Michigan

Michigan State and National Parks: A Complete Guide

Ultimate Michigan Adventures

Canoeing Michigan Rivers

Fish Michigan — 100 Southern Michigan Lakes

Fish Michigan — 100 Northern Lower Michigan Lakes

Fish Michigan — 100 Upper Peninsula Lakes

Fish Michigan — 50 Rivers

Fish Michigan — 50 More Rivers

Fish Michigan — 100 Great Lakes Hotspots

CONTENTS

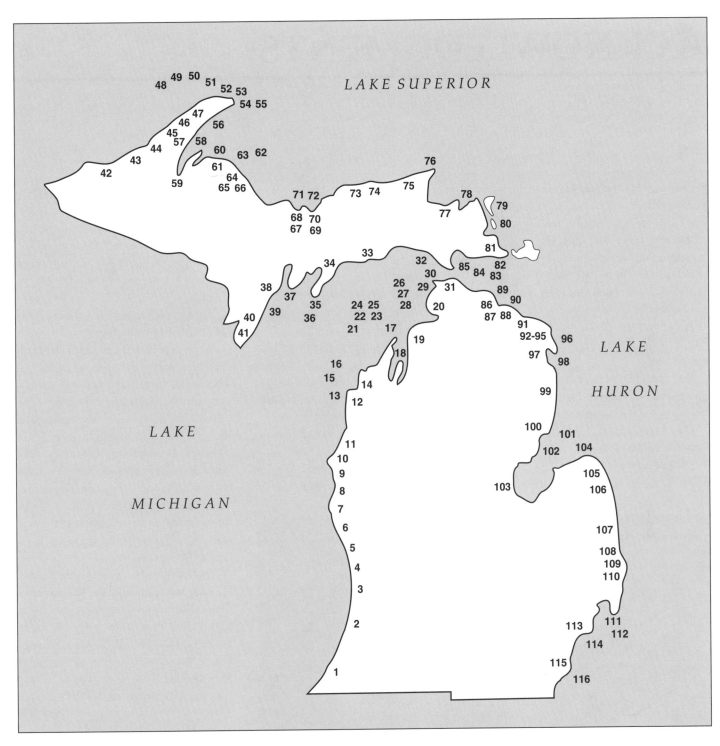

ACKNOWLEDGMENTS

In our travels from Isle Royale to downtown Detroit, we have met an extraordinary number of helpful and friendly people who generously gave of their time to help us in our search for Michigan's sweet-water lights. We would like to extend a sincere thank you to all of them, and especially:

Bob Nichols, *Director*, St. Joseph Public Library, for his help in the St. Joseph area.

Pete Sandman of the Frankfort-Elberta Chamber of Commerce for his help with several of the lights in his area.

David McCormick, for his help on the Grand Traverse Lighthouse.

Dick Moehl and his son Mike Moehl of Pinckney for an enjoyable trip to St. Helena Island.

Jack Edwards, *Scoutmaster* of Troop 4, Ann Arbor, for information on the Boy Scouts' role in the restoration of the St. Helena Island Lighthouse.

Pat Simons, for her special tour of the Ontonagon Lighthouse and also the information about her family's involvement as keepers of that light.

Dan Plescher and Bob Hill, Fort Wilkins State Park *Manager* and Assistant *Manager*, respectively, for special help in getting us to the Copper Harbor Lighthouse and the personal tour.

Pilot Steve Danforth, USAF Kincheloe AFB, Gwinn.

Dave Tinker of Sterling for taking us out to the Round Island Lighthouse on the St. Mary's River, even though the water was a little rough that day.

Diane McDonald and Bill Hansen for help with the Sturgeon Point Lighthouse.

Bob and Mary Schallip for help on the Neebish Island area of the St. Mary's River.

Robert and Karen Wiltse for the informative trip to Charity Island

We also would like to thank the many local historical societies that have had the foresight to protect and preserve the histories of the lightkeepers and their families and, in many cases, the lighthouses themselves. And everyone who loves lighthouses should be grateful to the Great Lakes Lighthouse Keepers Association, headquartered in Dearborn, whose members several years ago saw the need for an organization that could actively help preserve the important monuments to our past.

We also greatly appreciate the help of the men and women of the United States Coast Guard, who were always willing to take time to answer our many questions. Special thanks go to BM3 Mark Stevens, U.S. Coast Guard, St. Ignace, Michigan; M.A. Atkins, U.S. Coast Guard, Grand Haven, Michigan; and TWO 3 Stan Sitniewski, U.S. Coast Guard, Sault Ste. Marie, Michigan.

SOUTH MANITOU ISLAND LIGHT

FRONT COVER PHOTOS, clockwise from upper left: Pointe Aux Barques, p. 104, Sturgeon Point, p. 97, Big Sable Point, p. 10, and Old Mackinac Point, p. 33.

BACK COVER PHOTO: Little Sable Point, p. 7.

INTRODUCTION

Our family has always been fascinated with Michigan's history. But reading about history and actually seeing it firsthand are two very different experiences. Our goal in writing this book is not to try to bring history to life on these pages. There are already at least a dozen excellent books that detail the history of Michigan's and America's lighthouses.

Rather, our prime purpose, our main goal is to make it as easy as possible to get you out to these majestic, colorful and historical buildings, so that your own senses and imagination can do the rest. For two years, we traveled more than 20,000 miles, including 1,000 by boat, to personally view and photograph every Michigan lighthouse. We are pleased to share our experiences, so that you too can discover yet another of our state's wonders.

Their diverse settings make lighthouses outstanding destinations for all travelers. The sentinels stand at the edge of precipitous bluffs, nestle in soft dunes, perch at the end of long piers, hide on picturesque islands, and rise up from isolated shoals. Many of the beacons still guide ships through treacherous waters. Others have been abandoned, some to be later rescued by renovation and restoration. Several are open to the public, and a few include fascinating museums. Some of the most beautiful are centerpieces at Michigan's most-scenic state and local parks.

Lighthouses are not only architecturally beautiful and structurally unique. They also are fascinating monuments to a way of life that has vanished. With the rapid increase in technology, the simple task of putting match to wick was utterly lost. A visit to an old lighthouse can recall those simpler, yet very challenging times. If you are traveling with children, make a lighthouse part of your itinerary. Not only will they teach youngsters something about our history, but many also have beaches, picnic areas, and a variety of other family activities nearby.

You can visit lighthouses year round, and during the winter months, the ice and snow can make them exceptionally beautiful. At any time of year, lighthouses are magnets that attract the lenses of nearly all passing cameras.

Lights close to home make for excellent day trips. One of our family's favorites was to cruise along the Detroit River one afternoon to see the beautiful lights along its shore. For literally millions of people, this trip is just an hour away. No matter where you are in Michigan, you're never farther than 85 miles from a Great Lake. That means you're also never very far from a Michigan Great Lakes lighthouse.

Whether lighthouses have always been appealing to you, or whether you've never visited one, please use this book to get out into the beautiful Michigan countryside and begin to see and enjoy what history has left to us.

Just say Michigan. It says it all.

The Penrose Family
West Branch, Michigan

CAUTION

Walking to a lighthouse at the end of a pier or breakwall can be very pleasant and relaxing during good weather. But when waves wash over these structures, especially during high winds and storms, they become extremely dangerous. Footing is precarious, especially for children. So please use good judgment and caution when visiting those lights. During threatening weather, stay off breakwalls.

COURTESY

Some lighthouses are on private property and are even used as private residences. We urge you to be considerate and respect the rights of their owners. View them from a distance on public land or from the water, and when that is not possible, simply do not attempt to visit at all.

SEUL CHOIX LIGHT

PREFACE

Michigan is the only state bordered by four of the five Great Lakes, and its history has always been affected by those waters. During the 1600s the lakes and connecting waterways brought the first explorers and missionaries to the area. Later, *voyageurs* paddled their huge canoes, loaded with pelts, close to their shores. And during the early 1800s, many settlers from the east arrive here by ship.

But it wasn't until the Soo locks were completed in 1855 that the full power of Great Lakes transportation began to be felt. A few years before, Upper Peninsula iron and copper mines had begun to hint at the untold wealth buried beneath that part of the state. With the opening of the locks, the mines could ship in larger quanitites, and the delays while unloading and reloading for the portage around the St. Mary's Rapids became a problem of the past. Iron ore boats plus ships hauling lumber, building materials, and other products and merchandise to and from the major cities along the shores of the Great Lakes made for a major increase in lake traffic.

Paralleling the rapid increase in Great Lakes shipping was a growing need to mark points and harbors and warn of dangerous areas. George Washington created the U.S. Lighthouse Service in 1789, but Michigan didn't get its first lighthouse, the Fort Gratiot Light in Port Huron, until 1825. Other lights soon joined its ranks. A light was built on Bois Blanc Island in 1829, and the Thunder Bay Island Light near Alpena and St. Joseph Light at the southern shore of Lake Michigan both began shining in 1832. Lighthouses were then added by the dozens in each of the following several decades.

The light sources in those first beacons were wicks fueled by whale oil and, later, kerosene and acetylene. Around the turn of the century, electric-powered lamps began shining from the towers. The light beams were magnified by simple metal reflectors until the 1850s, when the Fresnel lens became the apparatus of choice around the lakes. The Waugoshance Light, in Michigan waters near the Straits of Mackinac, was the first on the Great Lakes to use the revolutionary arrangement of glass prisms that directed beacons much farther and brighter than before.

The wicks, lamps and lenses required "keepers" to light them at sunset, extinguish them at sunrise, and maintain them day-in and day-out during the shipping season. Lighthouses were the homes of not only the keepers, but often also their families. They were a unique breed of dedicated men and women, who often lived in isolated, lonely, sometimes primitive, and even dangerous conditions.

But in spite of their best efforts and the growing number of lights, far too many ships still ran aground or sank. So in the 1870s the U.S. Life Saving Service also began operations in Michigan. Each of the dozens of their stations was responsible for a specific section of coastline, and their crews regularly walked the shoreline to check for wreckage or other signs of trouble. When they noticed a ship coming too close to the shore, they fired flares into the air to warn the captain of the danger.

If a ship foundered near shore, the service men used a device called a Lyle gun, a small cannon that fired a small rope across the water to the stranded crews, who would then use it to haul over a much thicker line. The crew members on the disabled ship would then attach a type of sling called a "breeches buoy" to the line and ride it above the water safely to shore. (During the summer, you can see a demonstration of the breeches buoy at the Sleeping Bear Point Life Saving Museum, north of Empire.)

If disabled ships were not within reach of the Lyle gun, the Life Saving Service personnel themselves rowed out in boats to rescue shipwreck victims.

With the advent of motorized lifeboats and their greater range, the Life Saving stations were gradually abandoned, and by the end of World War II, most had disappeared. Many were part of lighthouse complexes, and today you can sometimes spot their remains. Footings, for instance, remain at Sand Point, next to the Pictured Rocks National Lakeshore office in Munising. And a few complete buildings stand near some lights, such as Point Betsie, Harbor Beach and Granite Island.

In the 1920s lightkeepers, themselves, began losing their jobs to automation. The keeper at the St. Helena Island Light was one of the first victims of the new technology. Acetylene gas was piped up to the light through a sensitive valve, which expanded with the heat of the day to stop the flow of gas and cooled off and contracted at night, allowing the gas to reach the pilot and ignite the light. Radio beacons were also added to many lights in the 1920s, and to help navigators even further, some lights synchronized their radio beacons with their fog horns.

In 1939 the Lighthouse Service was absorbed by the United States Coast Guard, and one by one Michigan lighthouses continued to be automated or

ROUND ISLAND (Straits of Mackinac) LIGHT

abandoned until 1983, when the last Michigan keeper, at Pt. Betsie, left his light. Today, solar-powered beacons, helicopters, fixed-wing aircraft, advanced radar, sonar and even satellites have taken us a long way from solitary watchmen walking the shores of the lake and lone figures dutifully climbing up towers to light wicks or lamps.

We will never know how many lives were saved due to the intervention of lightkeepers and lifesaving crews, but their efforts were remarkable. To most of them, their job was also a way of life, a way of life that has now nearly vanished.

But many of Michigan's remarkable lights are being helped by a new breed of lightkeeper — private citizens. Local historical societies, for instance, have been responsible for not only saving, but also restoring many lights. A group that is working very hard to preserve not only Michigan's but all of the Great Lakes historical lights is the Great Lakes Lighthouse Keepers Association headquartered at Henry Ford Estate, 4901 Evergreen Road, Dearborn, MI 48128.

The fate of the past is now in our hands, and what we do — or don't do — will determine what firsthand knowledge of lighthouses will be handed down to our children and to theirs. It's our decision.

ST. JOSEPH NORTH PIER LIGHTS

As the St. Joseph River empties into southern Lake Michigan, it divides the present-day communities of Benton Harbor and St. Joseph. As early as the 1830s, its strategic location made this area important to shipping concerns, and the crews of the ships that plied these waters appreciated any help the people on shore could give them. Legend has it that in the early 1800s one captain lived in a large house close to the lake here. Whenever he was expected to arrive in port, his family would hang lanterns in the second-story windows to help guide him safely home. Whether that story is true or not, the heavy lake traffic did make it necessary to erect a permanent light in the area.

In 1832 a lighthouse — the first

ST. JOSEPH INNER PIER

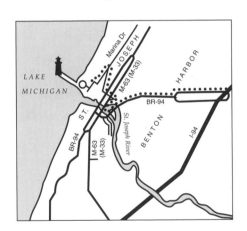

DIRECTIONS: From I-94 north of Benton Harbor, take S. Business Rte. 94 (exit 33) and drive about 5 miles to M-63 (called M-33 on older maps) in St. Joseph. Turn right (north) onto M-63, cross the St. Joseph River, and turn right (east) onto Upton Dr., the first road that intersects M-63 after you have crossed the bridge. Follow Upton, which curves sharply west then north, 0.6 miles to Marina Dr. Turn left (south) onto Marina (a brick road) and go 0.3 miles, around the west basin, to the entrance to Tiscornia Park, on the right. Follow the signs to the parking area. The pier and lighthouse are on the left.

Michigan light on Lake Michigan — was constructed on a bluff overlooking the lake. At about the same time the lighthouse was actually put into operation some 14 years later, a wood pier was built extending out into the lake, and a lighthouse was also erected at its end. In 1886 the light was increased with the installation of a Fresnel lens, and in 1907 the pier was extended and a steel outer light was added. The shore light continued in operation until 1924 then, unfortunately, was torn down in 1955.

Both pier lights, however, are still in operation, and today this is one of the few remaining pier range light systems on the Great Lakes. The outer light rests on a simple steel structure about 30 feet tall, but the inner light is housed in a much larger building. That steel-sided structure

rises two stories above the pier, its red hip roof contrasting with the crisp whiteness of the siding. An octagonal tower rises an additional two stories above the house and is topped by a black iron parapet and walkway. A catwalk, which extends the 300-plus yards from shore to the second story of the lighthouse, was built so that the keeper could attend to his duties even when angry waves were sweeping over the pier. The walkway continues on to the outer range light.

Today, a large area stretching north along the lake from the pier is set aside for public use as Tiscornia Park. You can stroll along the now-concrete pier or the sandy beach, and swimming is allowed, except near the pier. Other facilities at the park include a concession stand, public restrooms, and a picnic area.

2 SOUTH HAVEN SOUTH PIER LIGHT

Like the lights at St. Joseph, the South Haven light is perched at the end of a concrete pier that stretches several hundred feet out into the turquoise waters of Lake Michigan. Originally constructed in 1872 and rebuilt shortly after the turn of the century, the round, red steel structure is topped by a black parapet. When waves washed the pier, workers could reach the light by means of a catwalk that extends from shore out to the second story of the structure.

This light is a favorite with photographers, who like to visit close to sunset when they can silhouette a striking image in front of a blazing display of color.

The area surrounding the pier has been set aside as a public park with a picnic area, playground and concession stand.

The sandy beach is ideal for swimming, but there is no lifeguard.

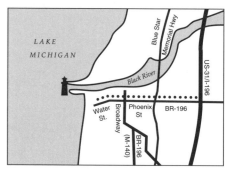

DIRECTIONS: From I-196 take exit 20 and follow Business Rte. 196 (Phoenix St.) west about one mile to where BR-196 turns left (south) onto Broadway St. Continue straight ahead (west) on Phoenix (which changes to Water St.) about 7 blocks to the south beach parking area. The south pier light is to the right of the parking area.

HOLLAND HARBOR LIGHTHOUSE 3

Thousands of people visit Holland, Michigan, each year, especially during its world-famous Tulip Festival. But most tourists leave without seeing one of the town's premier landmarks — the Holland Harbor Lighthouse, also known as "Big Red."

The large three-story building — topped by a gray-shingled roof and a square tower, which rises two additional stories — is set on a pier that runs along the south bank of a short channel connecting Lake Macatawa to Lake Michigan. The entire structure is painted bright red, and twin gables and diamond-paned windows add a unique touch to the architecture. To complete the picture of a grand American building, the stars and stripes ripples in the breeze above the tower. The original Fresnel lens is on display in the Holland Museum, at the corner of 10th Street and River Avenue.

A pier that stretches a little farther out into Lake Michigan from the lighthouse would seem to offer a good vantage point. But because of the difficulty in approaching that area and the lack of parking, we recommend that you view this lighthouse from a pier in busy Holland State Park, on the opposite (north) side of the river.

You can access that pier from Ottawa Beach, which also contains a playground, large picnic area, restrooms, changing rooms and a store. In some places just back from the excellent swimming beach, the low-lying dunes are topped with tufts of green shore grasses. Dune climbers can scramble up a large sand hill east of the parking area, and you can stroll along and even fish from the pier itself.

Or there's nothing more relaxing than to just pick out one of the many benches that line the channel, sit in the shade of a tree, and watch the river empty into Lake Michigan, while the red sentinel stands guard on the opposite shore.

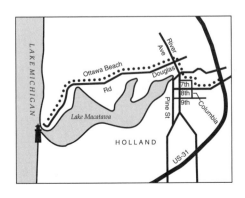

DIRECTIONS: From US-31 in Holland, turn west onto 8th St. (S. Business Rte 31) and go one mile to Columbia. Turn right (north) onto Columbia and go one block to 7th St. Turn left (west) onto 7th and go 3 blocks to River Ave. Turn right (north) onto River and go one mile to Douglas Ave. Turn left (west) onto Douglas (which changes to Ottawa Beach Rd.) and go 6 miles to Holland State Park's Ottawa Beach parking area. A daily or annual vehicle permit is required for entry.

On the return trip you will have to take a slightly different route through the downtown area. Retrace your path along Ottawa Beach Rd. (Douglas) back to River Ave. Turn right and follow River until you must bear right onto Pine St. Follow Pine to 9th St. turn left (east) onto 9th and go 4 blocks to Columbia. Turn left (north) onto Columbia and go one block to 8th. Turn right (east) onto 8th St. and follow it back to US-31.

4 GRAND HAVEN LIGHTS

As you gaze out across the wide expanse of never-ending sand at Grand Haven State Park, the blue of Lake Michigan is interrupted only by two small, red streaks to the north. They are the south pierhead light and the south pier inner light of Grand Haven, which stretch out into the water. For the convenience of the keepers who were assigned to this post in the past, a long catwalk joins both lights and also connects them to shore.

The inner light — originally built on shore in 1839, then moved and rebuilt in 1905 — is a 51-foot-tall, steel-sided near-cylindrical tower that has been painted fire-engine red, including the parapet and lantern room. Its companion light, at the end of the pier, is a square building, also painted red, with steel siding and a small tower that barely peeps over the roof line. It houses not only a light, but also a fog horn to assist mariners who are in the vicinity.

It's not until you walk around to the front of the building that you feel the full effect of its design. The structure rests on a huge, white concrete base, the front of which forms a sharp angle, like the prow of a land-bound ship pointed seaward. The white abutment, which dwarfs any-one who stands next to it, gives the impression that the lighthouse is casually biding its time, but ready, when it has to be, for any assault Lake Michigan may launch against it.

The pier makes a nice destination for a walk, and it's also an excellent place to fish. While we were there in late September, we saw many steelhead pulled from the waters, to the delight of both fisher-men and passersby.

The state park here has a campground right on the beach, a beautiful swimming area, a park store, restrooms and a bath-house. The extensive picnic area has a few shade trees and a large playground.

All in all, this is a great place to spend the day, with something for everyone.

DIRECTIONS: From US-31 in Grand Haven about one mile north of the south city limits sign, turn west onto Franklin Ave. (a one-way street west) and go 0.8 miles to South Harbor Dr. Turn left (south) onto South Harbor and go 0.9 miles to the Grand Haven State Park and lighthouse. On your return trip, follow South Harbor 2 blocks past Franklin to Columbus St. Turn right (east) onto Columbus, a one-way street east, and follow it back to US-31.

MUSKEGON SOUTH PIER LIGHT 5

From the shore of Lake Michigan near Muskegon, two concrete walls stretch out into the water, forming a perfect arc to protect the narrow strip of water that connects Lake Michigan to Muskegon Lake. Between those breakwaters, on the south side of the channel mouth, a short pier juts out into the Great Lake to form the base for the Muskegon South Pier Light.

The first light in this area was erected in 1851. The present-day light, built in 1903, is housed in a red, elongated steel-sided tower. Two smaller lights stand on the breakwaters farther out from shore. A white Coast Guard station marks the beginning of the pier, and directly south is Pere Marquette Park, with its sandy beach, bathhouse, picnic area and store.

Moored on the south side of the Muskegon Channel Wall at the park is the WWII submarine *U.S.S. Silversides*, a fascinating National Historic Landmark that is open to the public.

U.S. COAST GUARD STATION, MUSKEGON

DIRECTIONS: From US-31 at the point where it junctions with I-96, southeast of Muskegon, take N. Business Rte 31 (Seaway Dr.) west then north 4.2 miles to Sherman Blvd. Turn left (west) onto Sherman and go 3.2 miles to Beach St. Turn right (north) onto Beach and follow it 1.9 miles to the Pere Marquette Park parking area.

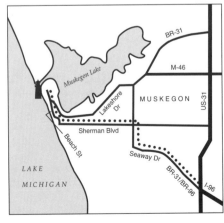

6 WHITE RIVER LIGHTHOUSE

White Lake is a long, narrow body of water that juts inland, and in 1870 commercial interests decided to cut a channel from its west shore to Lake Michigan. Five years later the mouth of that channel became the site of what is now called the White River Light Station.

The lighthouse is tucked snugly between the channel on the north, the nearby Lake Michigan shore on the west, and towering hills on the south. An expansive, shade-dappled lawn sprawls to a wood fence that serves as a divider between the lighthouse and the channel. Thick bushes cover the steep hill from the fence down to the water's edge, and Victorian-style iron lamp posts border walkways that lead from the parking area to the lighthouse.

The lighthouse, which is constructed of light-colored brick, includes many unique architectural details. Brick abutments give support to the tower structure, and the white trim on the house is uncommon and deserving of a second look. Wild vines stretch upward to partly cover the face of the eight-sided tower. And look closely for pink geraniums that peek out through the small windows.

Inside, you can stroll through a fine nautical museum, which includes the Fourth Order Fresnel lens originally used at this location. You can also climb a beautiful iron staircase into the light tower for a sprawling view of Lake Michigan and bordering sand dunes.

The museum is open Memorial Day weekend through Labor Day, Tuesday through Friday, 11 a.m. to 5 p.m., and weekends, noon to 6 p.m. During September the museum is open on weekends from noon to 6 p.m.

DIRECTIONS: From US-31 east of Whitehall, exit onto White Lake Dr. and follow it west 4.4 miles to South Shore Rd. Turn left (south) onto South Shore and go 3.7 miles (at 1.6 miles the route makes a brief jog west on Lakewood St.) to a four-way stop. Look for a lighthouse museum sign straight across the intersection. Continue straight ahead and follow the road (Murray Rd.) one mile. As you approach the end of the road, look for a driveway, marked by a lighthouse sign, on the left. Follow that narrow road about one block to the lighthouse and gift shop parking area. *We advise against taking trailers or large RVs to this area.*

LITTLE SABLE POINT LIGHT 7

The Little Sable Light is one of the most beautiful lights along the shores of Lake Michigan. The narrow, conical tower stretches more than 100 feet into the deepening blue of sunny skies, and its smooth brick takes on a russet hue as the sun dips into the west. A black cast-iron parapet with curved supports crowns the structure with elegance. Low bushes hide the base, and large rocks have been scattered in front of the light to prevent erosion. The beauty of the structure is enhanced by its surroundings, The tower stands in a remote section of Silver Lake State Park that is covered by dunes, including several large ones a few hundred yards inland from the light. Small greenery clings tenaciously to the dune slopes, and from the parking area you pass through an avenue of Lombardy poplar that guides you directly to the light and a wide stretch of cool, sandy Lake Michigan beach.

Far from any town, Little Sable Point was a lonely post when manned, and today, when no one calls it home, it seems even more so. The only evidence that this place was once lived in is the foundation of the keeper's house, which peeks through the sand a few feet from the tower.

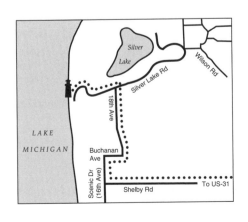

DIRECTIONS: From US-31 at Shelby, exit onto Shelby Rd. and go west 6.3 miles to Scenic Dr. (16th Ave.) Turn right (north) onto Scenic and follow the paved road, which changes to Buchanan then 18th Ave., about 3.5 miles to where it deadends at Silver Lake Rd. Turn left (west) onto Silver Lake Rd. and go 0.6 miles to where the road jogs sharply north. Turn left (west) onto a narrow, curvy gravel road and follow it about ½ mile to the light tower parking area. This is a state park fee area.

8 PENTWATER PIER LIGHTS

The Pentwater North and South Pier Lights stand at the mouth of the Pentwater River, which forms the south boundary of Charles Mears State Park, in Pentwater. The south breakwater's smooth concrete supports the red-and-white steel skeleton of a light tower that rises about 25 feet above the water. Across the river on the north pier is an equally tall, circular light tower whose smooth, white and functional metal siding encloses a foghorn.

At Mears State Park, a beautiful white-sand beach stretches several hundred yards north from the north pier. Nestled in the dunes behind the north half of the beach is a 180-site campground. Back from the water on the south end of the park is a day-use area with a swimming beach, playground, restrooms, concession stand, and a few widely scattered picnic tables under shade trees.

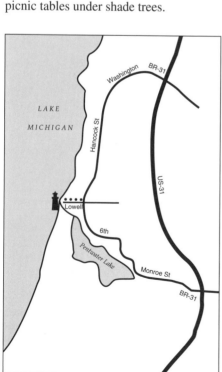

NORTH PIER LIGHT

SOUTH PIER LIGHT

 DIRECTIONS: From US-31 near Pentwater, exit onto either North Business Rte 31 (Monroe, 6th then Hancock streets) or South Business Rte. 31 (Washington then Hancock streets) and follow either route a little more than 3 miles to Lowell St. Turn west onto Lowell and go 0.3 miles to Charles Mears State Park. A daily or annual permit is required for entrance. The pier lights are at the south end of the beach area.

LUDINGTON NORTH PIERHEAD LIGHT

The Ludington Pierhead Light is a three-story pyramid-shaped tower at the edge of the pier in Ludington Harbor. The white steel-sided tower rests off-center on a large, black concrete base that angles sharply toward the side of the pier. A small stairway allows you to walk around one side of the structure.

In August 1994, as the light was being worked on, it suddenly settled six inches to one side. There are no immediate plans to repair the slight list.

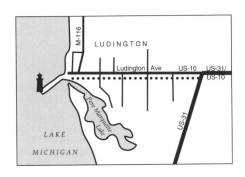

DIRECTIONS: From the junction of US-31 and US-10 just east of Ludington, go west on US-10 (Ludington Ave.) about 3.7 miles to the end of the road, at Stearns Park.

10 BIG SABLE POINT LIGHTHOUSE

Big Sable Point Lighthouse is a mysterious, yet inviting place to visit. The beauty of the dunes angling down to meet the azure water, the white-caps appearing out of nowhere to rush toward shore, and, yes, the absence of people, combine to make this a very exclusive and enjoyable destination.

The light at Big Sable Point is the last Michigan beacon seen by ships veering southward farther from shore to the port of Chicago, and it is the first spotted on their trip up the lake. For something so important, it is painful to see Big Sable — now automated — as abandoned as it is today. Yet at the same time, this desolation seems at home in the shifting sands of the great dunes that surround it.

The 1.5-mile walk to the lighthouse from the campground in Ludington State Park is an easy one, along a hard-packed sandy road lined with scrub pines and small hardwoods. The route parallels the Lake Michigan shoreline, and as you move through the area's dunes, the tall, black-and-white tower begins to peer out over the sandy expanse.

It isn't until you get closer to the house and tower, however, that you begin to see the obvious signs of disrepair. White paint is crumbling off the house, exposing patches of brown brick. Concrete sidewalks around the base of the light tower have cracked and fallen in large slabs, and the asphalt that once paved the drive has been reduced to rubble. Pieces of mortar and bits of brick are scattered around the grounds, and a few foundations of long-forgotten buildings are still visible, while others have been eaten up by the ever-shifting dunes.

The basic structure of the lightkeeper's dwelling, however, has survived the ravages of time with its dignity intact. The windows are still in place, the roof is sound, and the foundation has suffered minimal damage.

The sturdy tower, too, has withstood the elements fairly well. Around the turn of the century, small steel-plate rectangles were artfully pieced together to encase and protect the tower's deteriorating brick and watchroom. The white metal wrap was painted in 1989 with a wide, black center band.

The lighthouse and gift shop are open to the public May 1 through October, daily from 10 a.m. to 6 p.m., and for a small fee you can also climb the tower during those hours. Three times a year the lighthouse holds an open house, with scheduled bus tours offering visitors the opportunity to be driven to the door of the light (saving a 3-mile round-trip walk). For schedules and further information call (616) 845-7343 during the seasonal business hours.

The Third Order Fresnel lens from this light is on display at the White Pine Village, south of Ludington.

For information on helping to preserve this light, contact the Big Sable Point Lighthouse Association, P.O. Box 673, Ludington, MI 49431.

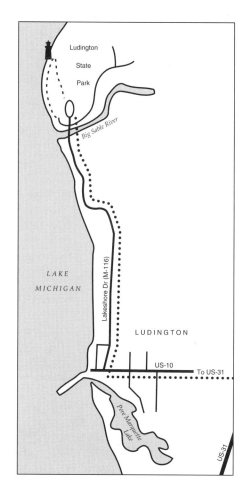

DIRECTIONS: From the junction of US-31 and US-10 just east of Ludington, go west on US-10 (Ludington Ave.) about 3.6 miles to M-116 (Lakeshore Dr.) Turn left (north) onto M-116 and go 6.4 miles to the entrance to Ludington State Park. An annual or daily sticker is required for entry. From the registration building, continue straight ahead to the first intersection after you cross the Big Sable River. Continue straight a few yards to the parking area for the Lighthouse Trail. The trailhead is about a block away, at the north end of the campground, at a green gate between lots 74 and 75. Follow the trail about ½ mile to a yellow gate, and from there it is about one more mile to the lighthouse.

An alternate route is to turn left at the intersection after crossing the river and go about a block to the beach house parking area. From there you can walk north up the beach a little more than 1.5 miles to the lighthouse.

BIG SABLE POINT LIGHTHOUSE

11 MANISTEE NORTH PIERHEAD LIGHT

Two piers extend into Lake Michigan from the mouth of the Manistee River, at Manistee. Set at the end of the north pier is a 39-foot-tall, white, conical steel tower, whose light still shines out over the nearby environs of Lake Michigan. A recently restored catwalk, which stretches from shore about 300 yards to the side of the structure, provided past keepers with easier access during rough weather and icy storms.

Two beautiful parks, including beaches — one on each side of the river here — make this a wonderful place to spend the day. The 5th Ave. Beach and Park, on the north shore, offers restrooms, concessions, a playground and changing rooms. A lifeguard is on duty at scheduled times. On the opposite shore, the First Street Beach and Park is similar, but with a larger expanse of lawn for family picnics and games, plus a pavilion for public use.

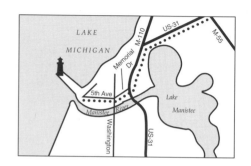

DIRECTIONS: From the junction of M-55 and US-31, east of Manistee, go west then south on US-31 approximately 1.6 miles to Memorial Dr., the last street before crossing the Manistee River. Turn right (west) onto Memorial, which changes to 5th Ave. at a blinking light, and go one mile to the beach parking area.

FRANKFORT NORTH BREAKWATER LIGHT 12

The Frankfort North Breakwater Light is a two-story-high, square, white steel-sided tower. This station has never been manned, but a door halfway up the landward side of the light suggests that a catwalk once led out from shore. The pier is a popular destination for walkers in the area, and there is a nice beach area nearby, with a playground.

An additional point of nautical interest, the *City of Milwaukee* is anchored across the bay from the light. The ship is one of the few remaining train ferries that, for the first half of the century, regularly carried railroad cars and passengers across Lake Michigan between Michigan and Wisconsin. The Society for the Preservation of the *City of Milwaukee* (2956 Glory Rd., Frankfort, MI 49635) is planning to restore the vessel.

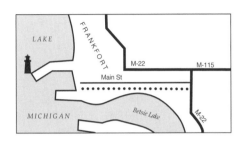

DIRECTIONS: From the junction of M-115 and M-22, go one block south on M-22 to Main St. Turn right (west) onto Main and go about ½ mile to the beach and parking area.

13 POINT BETSIE LIGHTHOUSE

For mariners Point Betsie is a very important light because it marks the spot where ships begin to turn toward or from the Manitou Passage. Built in 1858, it wasn't fully automated until 1983, making it the last manned lighthouse on mainland Michigan. Today, motors turn the original gearworks, and the facility no longer houses Coast Guard families.

Built on a slight rise in the sandy shoreline and guarded by a row of towering Lombardy poplar on a small ridge to the south, the lighthouse has a commanding view of the area. The pristine-white dwelling is topped with a red-shingled barn-style roof that sharply contrasts with the blue of sunny skies. The large (nearly 30 by 50 feet) two-story house easily accommodates two families comfortably. Second-story windows peek out from under red-shingled dormers, and twin covered porches provide the perfect evening gathering place for residents seeking the lake's sweet breezes.

The round three-story tower is attached to the house, so keepers were

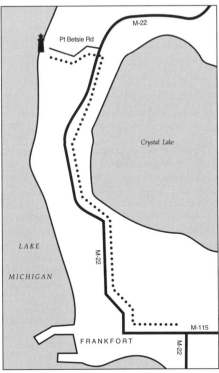

impervious to any rough weather that might howl outside. The white steel-sided tower is just tall enough to peep out over the roofline of the house, and its parapet is capped in red to match the larger building.

In an effort to deter the powerful force of the lake, steel breakwaters encased in cement were constructed from the base of the tower toward the lake. If you are standing on one of the walls when the water is rough, you can feel the cement shake as the waves crash against it. Watching the waves here can be hypnotic, as they crest and break against the wall, sending a shower of thousands of droplets over you.

South of the lighthouse are two aban-doned structures: a life-saving station and another old Coast Guard building. Still standing is the life-saving station's tower, where for the first third of this century, men stood during exhausting watches, searching the horizon for ships in distress.

 DIRECTIONS: From the junction of M-115 and M-22, go west then north on M-22 approximately 5.6 miles to Pt. Betsie Rd. Turn left (west) onto Pt. Betsie Rd. and go about 0.7 miles to its end. The lighthouse is on the right, the abandoned Coast Guard buildings on the left.

14 ROBERT H. MANNING MEMORIAL LIGHT

In 1991 a new light was added to the list of Michigan's old beauties, most of which have stood for several generations and several for more than a century. When the Robert H. Manning Memorial Light was dedicated and lit on the shores of Lake Michigan near Empire, it became not only Michigan's newest light, but also only the second memorial light in the state.

The light, which sits on a beautiful beach overlooking the whitecaps as they sweep to shore, is a touching tribute to Robert Manning, a lifelong resident of Empire. Manning's passion was fishing. Whenever possible he headed out into Lake Michigan, and after just about every late-evening return, he would good-naturedly remark that a lighthouse at Empire sure would help him find his way home more easily.

After Manning died at age 62 in 1989, his family decided to honor him by building the light he had for so long. Family funds plus contributions from the townspeople and other sources turned the fisherman's wish into reality. In 1991 the Manning Memorial Light began shining, and the Coast Guard will soon add it to their official nautical charts.

The light is housed in a small, round three-story tower that rests on an octagonal foundation with steps leading up to the door of the light. The wood door and the windows that stretch above it are painted gray, which blends with the crisp white of the stucco tower. Ridges near the top gradually widen to accommodate the black parapet, and the lantern room is enclosed by narrow panes of glass from top to bottom. A gold ventilator ball caps the structure, which has an understated beauty that will last for years.

A park, with a sandy beach that stretches along the shore, surrounds the tower. Facilities include changing rooms, restrooms, a large picnic area, and both a basketball and a volleyball court.

Empire is located in the center of Sleeping Bear Dunes National Lakeshore, and the headquarters building, which has a maritime museum, is only a half mile from the Manning Light. Also, the Sleeping Bear Point Life Saving Station and museum is just a few miles drive north.

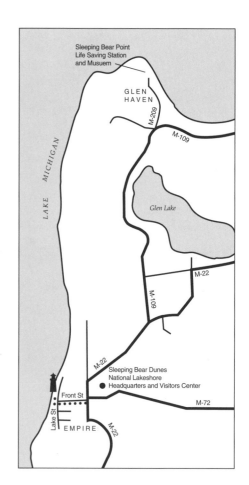

SLEEPING BEAR POINT LIFE SAVING STATION BOAT HOUSE

DIRECTIONS: From the intersection of M-72 and M-22, go west on Front St. 3 blocks to its end at Lake St. Turn right (north) onto Lake and follow it (it jogs left after a block) about 0.2 miles to the parking area at Empire Beach. The lighthouse is at the north end of the park.

The Sleeping Bear National Lakeshore visitors center and museum is on M-72 one block east of the M22/M-72 junction.

To get to the Sleeping Bear Point Life Saving Station and museum, go north on M-22 from the M-72/M-22 junction approximately 2 miles to M-109. M-22 jogs east at this junction. Continue straight (north) on M-109 and go 4.4 miles to M-209. M-109 turns sharply right at this junction. Continue straight ahead on M-209 0.4 miles to Sleeping Bear Rd., at the beach area. (In this stretch you may be able to see North Manitou Shoal Light, far out in the water. This is as close as you can get to it from land.) Turn left (west) onto Sleeping Bear Rd. and go ½ mile to the museum parking area.

ROBERT H. MANNING MEMORIAL LIGHT

15 SOUTH MANITOU ISLAND LIGHTHOUSE

16 NORTH MANITOU ISLAND SHOAL LIGHT

The Manitou Islands, which lie clearly visible nearly seven miles offshore, are among Michigan's best places to "get away from it all."

To some the ferry ride, alone, is worth a visit. The Manitou Island Transit Company, in Leland, makes one daily run to South Manitou Island in the morning, then returns about four hours after its arrival. During the hour-and-a-half ride, you glide past the majestic beauty of Sleeping Bear Dunes National Lakeshore, which includes both North and South Manitou islands. To the south the towering dunes on the mainland seem to slip beneath the crisp blues of Lake Michigan, and in front of the ferry's bow, the islands loom up through the haze.

The narrow Manitou Passage, which runs between the islands and the mainland, is one of the most dangerous on the Great Lakes. Ships have to make several turns here, and because of the shoals surrounding the islands, precision is critical. In the past, in addition to the islands' two lights, the South Manitou Life Saving Station and the Sleeping Bear Point Lifesaving Station, on the mainland about halfway between Leland and Empire, also stood ready to assist any vessel that foundered.

North Manitou Island Shoal Light stands in the Manitou Passage, atop the hazardous shoal itself, surrounded by water. The ferry passes close to this structure, which in 1935 replaced a light (no longer standing) that had operated on the island's shore since 1898. From 1910 to 1927 a lightship also helped mark the treacherous area.

The automated beacon of the current light still guides ships up and down the passage between the Manitous and the mainland. A huge, square concrete base firmly anchors a smaller, square five-story tower. Nearly 60 winters of ice have chipped, deeply gouged and scarred the once-smooth concrete base, and rust marks cover its white sides. North Manitou Island, itself, is 15,000 acres of totally undeveloped wilderness.

The slender spire of the South Manitou Island Lighthouse dominates the shoreline to the south of the harbor, on the island's east shore, where the ferry docks. This, the only natural harbor between here and Chicago, was once a scheduled stopping place for steamers that chugged up Lake Michigan. The ships would lay over just long enough to replenish their supply of hardwood fuel and then take off again.

It's an easy quarter-mile walk from the ferry dock to the lighthouse along a path that, when it reaches the beach, is covered by boards, both to make walking on the sandy shoreline easier and also to protect the area's fragile dune environment. The boardwalk ends at two white buildings with red roofs that sit near the shore. A winding path leads from them up to the main point of interest, the lighthouse and tower, which are situated on the crest of a dune that rises about 30 feet from the blue waters below.

Built in 1871 to replace earlier structures, the brick house, painted pale yellow, rests on a foundation of thick, white stone walls. Decorative arches curve over the doorways and windows, and borders of bushes and wild grasses leave slashes of green across the stark-white foundation. A narrow, enclosed passageway, its roofline a story lower than that of the dwelling, connects the house and tower.

The 100-foot-tall, round tower is also constructed of brick. A few small windows are scattered up along its staircase, and near the top a row of four arched windows circles the tower between a narrow, black painted band and the parapet. The black cast-iron walkway and its supports provide a strong balance for the grand expanse of whiteness below them. This light and its surroundings are uncommonly beautiful and must have pleased many of its residents over the years.

One was Dr. Alonzo Slyfield, who

SOUTH MANITOU ISLAND LIGHTHOUSE

became keeper of this light in 1853. It's easy for most people to think that the men and women who kept Michigan's lights burning did little more than wearily trudge up and down winding stairs with their lanterns swaying. But when a call of distress came in, very often the keepers were called upon to help in rescues. For instance, during one particularly busy day, Dr. Slyfield — the only doctor ever to reside on the island — interrupted his medical and lightkeeping duties to save the lives of several men and women who clung to a capsized boat.

Today, when you travel along the island's overgrown roads past long-abandoned farmsteads and old cemeteries, you can't help but feel that for residents, life here has never been easy.

But for visitors the island has something for explorers of just about every age and inclination. Miles of trails that crisscross the interior, plus the beautiful sand beaches that circle the island make this an ideal location to hike and backpack. Overnighters have their choice of three primitive campgrounds. A virgin forest on the southern shore is home to the world's largest white cedar, more than 17 feet in diameter and well over five centuries. old. Nearby, the wreck of the huge freighter *Francisco Morazan* protrudes from the shallow water in graphic testimony to the need for the area's lights.

Because the fragile environment here must be protected, nothing with wheels is allowed on the island, including not only cars, but also bicycles and wagons. The only exceptions are tour vehicles, which are allowed to run along the main roads. The guided tours, which last about an hour and a half, are the only way to take in everything on the island quickly.

Unfortunately, the four hours between the ferry's arrival and departure are just barely enough time to explore the lighthouse and the buildings farther inland. And unless you've made overnight plans at one of the campgrounds, don't be tempted to overstay the departure time. Time, tide, and the Manitou Island Ferry wait for no one, which some travelers have found out the hard way.

NORTH MANITOU ISLAND SHOAL LIGHT

DIRECTIONS: From M-22 in Leland, turn west onto River St., the first street north of the river, and go 2 blocks to the last building on the left. In the gift shop there, you can purchase boat tickets and get directions to a ferry-boat parking area. A shuttle bus will pick you up at the parking area and take you back to your vehicle when you return from the island.

For a current schedule and passage, write Manitou Island Transit, P.O. Box 591, Leland, MI 49654 or phone (616) 256-9061 or (616) 271-4217.

GRAND TRAVERSE LIGHTHOUSE 17

Grand Traverse Lighthouse, also known as Cat's Head, was first erected in 1851. The remaining lighthouse is no longer in service, and its empty tower, other buildings and land are now a part of Leelanau State Park. A new light sits on a steel frame farther out on the tip of land — the "little finger" of Michigan's "mitten" — that stretches out into Lake Michigan and marks the entrance to Grand Traverse Bay. The new light's steel panels have been painted with a white-and-red diamond pattern, but it still is just a functional tool, without a fraction of the charm of the huge, white house behind it.

Fortunately, the Grand Traverse Lighthouse is not another discarded remnant of a bygone era that has outworn its usefulness. The lighthouse is now a museum, which serves as a beacon

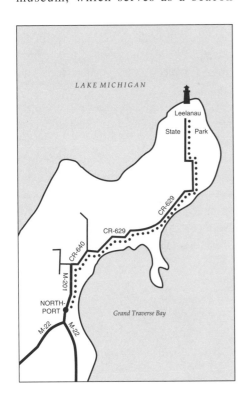

DIRECTIONS: From the junction of M-22 and M-201 in Northport, take M-201 through the town as follows: go north 0.2 miles to the blinker light; turn right, onto Main, and go one block; turn left, onto Wakazoo, and go one long block; turn right, onto Nagonaba, and go one block; turn left, onto Mill Rd., and go 1.1 miles. When you reach the city limits, the road changes to County Rd. 640, then 1.3 miles farther it changes to County Rd. 629. Follow CR-629 5.3 miles to Leelanau State Park. An annual or daily permit is required to enter. The lighthouse and gift shop parking area are just inside the park entrance.

David McCormick, who retired after a 30-year career in the U.S. Coast Guard, is the current caretaker of the Grand Traverse Lighthouse. His father, James McCormick, was the keeper at this lighthouse from 1922 to 1939 and built the stone planter shown below.

attracting anyone interested in Michigan's history. Its beauty has been touchingly preserved. Inside, early photos of the site and antique furnishings, toys and kitchenware make it very easy to imagine what life would have been like at this solitary station.

The large, two-story brick house is situated on a beautiful expanse of lawn that stretches toward the lake. Large trees — almost as tall as the light tower, which rises up from the top of the house's red-shingled gable roof — shade and help cool the dwelling in the warm months. Flowering shrubs dot the manicured lawn, and beautiful stone planters that were hand-crafted by James McCormick, a lightkeeper here, are still filled with colorful blossoms during the summer.

A narrow sidewalk, which runs the length of the yard down toward the water, passes a red brick building originally built to house the kerosene and other paraphernalia necessary for operating the light. All flammables were required to be housed in buildings such as these, a policy that still makes sense nearly a century after it was first put into practice.

Toward the rocky lakeshore, grasses peek out in thick bundles around the stones. Down the shoreline itself, a fence separates the lawn from the wild tangle of brush on the other side, and beyond a patch of forest is a state park campground, which is very popular during the summer.

The museum and gift shop are open May 1 through October, noon to 5 p.m. daily.

The Grand Traverse Lighthouse Foundation encourages and welcomes volunteers and new members. Contact them by writing to P.O. Box 43, Northport, MI 49760; phoning (616) 386-7195; or e-mailing gtlthse@gtii.com.

OLD MISSION POINT LIGHTHOUSE 18

The lighthouse on Old Mission Point is as intriguing as its name implies. The short path from the parking area to the shore leads through dense hardwoods filled with vibrant shades of green. The thick woods rush toward the water, then stop abruptly just as they reach the sandy beach. The beach is unusual in that although it is entirely sand, at the water line, rocks begin to appear throughout the shallows and poke up out of the water in a bumpy display. There's room for swimming and wading, though, and the bottom is sandy, not the expected jumble of gravel. A few picnic tables are scattered back from the beach area.

Built in 1870, this small, beautiful lighthouse is still in good condition. A sturdy, unpainted fence that surrounds the building gives it a solid border of gray. The wood house is painted white, and a small, white tower peeks up from the crest of the roofline. The parapet is black cast iron. This is no longer a working light. The lens has been removed to another location and the lantern room is empty. The building is not open to the public.

We visited Old Mission Point on a drizzly gray day. As we approached the shore, wisps of fog rolled in, hiding all but a few large rocks far out in the water.

But what a sight greeted us — the lighthouse, its stark whiteness contrasting with the heavy greens of the forest on all sides, guarding the expanse of water it faced with an air of gentle power. Although most of our visits to lights had been made in the bright sunlight, we realized that when the weather turns and the force of nature attacks these structures with rain, waves and ice, the true strength of a lighthouse shines through.

DIRECTIONS: From the junction of M-37 and US-31 on the east side of Traverse City, follow M-37 north approximately 17 miles to its end, at the parking area for the Old Mission Point Lighthouse.

19 CHARLEVOIX SOUTH PIER LIGHT

The Charlevoix South Pierhead Light is anchored on a small, square tower at the end of a concrete pier just a little more than 100 feet from shore. The steel-frame tower is open at its bottom third and enclosed by metal plates at the top. A solar panel on the front of the tower is the power source for the automated light, and a small ladder, which provides access for maintenance, steps up to a door on the middle of the landward side. Huge, white boulders that surround the narrow pier keep the worst of the waves away from the concrete footings.

Just south of the pier is a sandy swimming beach with a playground.

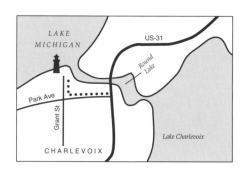

DIRECTIONS: From US-31 in downtown Charlevoix, turn west onto Park Ave., the first street south of the drawbridge over the Pine River, and go approximately 0.3 miles to Grant St. Turn right (north) onto Grant and go one block to the beach parking area.

20 LITTLE TRAVERSE LIGHTHOUSE

Little Traverse (Harbor Point) Lighthouse is not open to the public, and access by land is cut off by a series of gates and guards. It is possible to view the light from the waters of Little Traverse Bay off Harbor Point. During the summer months, the *Bay Pride* ferry offers nautical tours out of Petoskey that include brief but close-up views of this lighthouse. Phone (231) 347-5550 for a schedule and further information.

SOUTH FOX ISLAND LIGHTHOUSE 21

Between North Manitou Island and Beaver Island, two much smaller pieces of land — North and South Fox islands — rise above the otherwise unbroken surface of Lake Michigan. Though both are privately owned, the lighthouse and a small parcel of land on South Fox Island is government-owned. There is no ferry service to the island, however, and the only way to visit this remote area is by boat or to fly over it in a plane.

We chose the latter, and 20 minutes after taking off from Traverse City Airport, the lush green of South Fox Island loomed into view. A thick carpet of trees covers the island, and one of only two breaks in the forest is a small section near shore that has been cleared for an air strip and several buildings. The runway is privately owned and marked with white crosses, which means it's unsafe for use.

The small peninsula at the south end of the island is home to the lighthouse. There, the second break in the forest, a large swath of sandy dunes, divides the peninsula from the rest of the island. But then the green thickness resumes almost to the water's edge, where a narrow strip of pale sand protects the trees from the powerful waves. The shoreline is particularly beautiful from the air, since the water deepens only gradually. Whitecaps chase one another to shore on all three sides of the sharply angled peninsula.

In the middle of the small peninsula forest stands the old South Fox Island Lighthouse. No longer in use, the square, white tower and attached dwelling have been boarded up against the elements, improving their chances at survival. A nearby brick building has been treated in a similar manner. Much closer to the shore near the peninsula's tip, the new tower rises to survey the turquoise waters below. That very narrow, circular tower is topped with a wider, black walkway, lantern room and green cap. A steel skeleton surrounds the tower to give it a firm support. A small house sits at the base of the light near the shore, hidden behind the thick trees.

22 BEAVER ISLAND HARBOR LIGHT

23 BEAVER HEAD LIGHTHOUSE

You can't write about Beaver Island without mentioning its most bizarre resident — the infamous James Jesse Strang. In 1850 Strang, a Mormon convert, began a small community of the religion's followers on Beaver Island and declared himself their king. Through manipulation, threat and fear, King Strang urged his subjects to follow his lead in attacking and stealing from the Gentile residents not only on Beaver Island but also other nearby islands. His raids took him as far north as St. Helena Island, where he harassed and stole several items from the lighthouse keeper and

BEAVER ISLAND HARBOR LIGHT

his family. In 1856 Strang was assassinated, ending what was the only absolute monarchy ever within the United States.

Another of the island's fascinating, though less-well-known and more-respected residents was Elizabeth Whitney Van Riper. Her husband became keeper of the lighthouse on St. James Harbor in 1869, but like so many of his fellow keepers, he later perished while trying to rescue people from a boat that had gone down in the area. Instead of being overcome by the tragedy, Elizabeth applied to continue on as keeper of the harbor light. Her request was granted, and she performed her duties with great care. In 1884 she married Daniel Williams, and they moved to the mainland to the Harbor Point Light, which guards Little Traverse Bay. While serving as keeper there, she wrote a fascinating autobiography of her life on the Great Lakes titled, *Child of the Sea*.

All that remains of the Beaver Island Harbor Light (also known as the St. James Harbor Light) that Van Riper tended is the small, two-story brick tower, which still stands on a narrow peninsula that juts out into the water near the edge of town. The white, cylindrical structure is capped by a black cast iron parapet. A small window near the top looks out over the green branches of a few large trees nearby.

On the southern end of the island, the Beaver Head Lighthouse stands as a

monument to hard work and perseverance. Restoration of the structure is one of the ongoing projects included in a state-run program called the Youth Employment Training Project. Directors and participants come from the Charlevoix Community School District, and students can receive credit for time spent working on the project. During the school year, young people repoint brick, paint the exterior, and refurbish and restore the interior.

The keeper's brick house, painted light yellow, rests on an old yet solid foundation of large field stones. Though the house could easily accommodate two families, a second two-story house was added onto the back of the structure. That white wood-sided dwelling includes a back porch just right for catching the breezes that drift across the island. A narrow one-story corridor of light-colored brick stretches from the first house to the light tower itself. Random, incongruous red bricks freckle the conical tower's pale-brown brick up to the black parapet and walkway.

The structure sits on a bluff high above Lake Michigan, and during the summer months, from 8 a.m. to 9 p.m., you can climb up the tower for a beautiful view of the emerald waters stretching out below. While gazing down the shoreline in both directions through the surrounding heavy forest, with the sound of the waves crashing below, it's hard not to

BEAVER HEAD LIGHTHOUSE

be impressed, even overcome, by the natural simplicity of the place. Old-fashioned streetlights are still intact, the manicured lawn is dotted with several large shrubs and a few hardwoods, and an old oil tank still rests on its cradle in the yard. Steps lead down several steep inclines, and a footpath makes its way down to the shore.

You can reach both of the island's lighthouses by car. If you haven't brought your own vehicle over on the ferry, you can rent a jeep, golf cart or bicycle in St. James. Hikers have their choice of several trails, which stretch into the interior, pass several inland lakes, and lead to miles of isolated sandy beaches. Charter boats are available, and this archipelago includes at least seven other islands near enough to visit.

For an excellent description of all the facilities and attractions on Beaver Island, see *Natural Michigan*, by Tom Powers.

DIRECTIONS: You can reach the island by either car ferry or regularly scheduled airplane flights, both out of Charlevoix. The 18-minute flight costs about $50 per person; the ferry ride takes about 3½ hours and costs approximately $100 for a family of four and their vehicle.

Ferries depart at least once a day from the Beaver Island Boat dock, on the east side of US-31, just south of the drawbridge in downtown Charlevoix. If you are taking a vehicle to the island, reservations are a must, and are recommended either way. For a current ferry schedule and rates, call (616) 547-2311.

The Island Airways flights lift off from Charlevoix Municipal Airport, on US-31 just south of the M-66 junction. For flight information call (616) 547-2141.

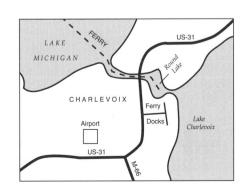

24 SQUAW ISLAND LIGHTHOUSE

On tiny Squaw Island, the northernmost in the Beaver Island archipelago, is one of the most architecturally beautiful of all Michigan lighthousess. Sadly, the value of this precious gem has been overlooked, and only a few years separate it from total obscurity and ruin.

Constructed of chocolate-colored brick, the house supports a red-shingled roof that angles sharply down from high gables past second-story border windows to the first-story wall. Rickety stairs climb through overgrown shrubs to a covered porch that fills an L-notch in the front of the house. A small wood railing runs between decorative wood supporting columns.

Builders used brick to the best advantage, and both the house and attached tower are filled with the small details of master craftsmen. Delicate brick arches curve over the house windows, and white stone sills support them. The square base of the brick tower juts into the main house at an angle. Buttresses support the heavy sides, and two arched windows match those on the house. Above the second story, the tower becomes octagonal in shape, with several porthole-shaped windows — trimmed and connected by raised, decorative brick borders — just below the walkway. Black cast iron creates the walkway, and the lantern room is still intact.

Inside, hardwood trim lines the doors and windows, and sturdy steps lead up to the second story. The buildings appear to be structurally sound, and it's likely that little major renovation would be needed to restore the interior. One of the reasons this priceless light isn't in even worse condition is that, being so far from the mainland, it has at least escaped destruction by graffiti artists and other vandals.

Recently a civic-minded carpenter volunteered supplies and labor to seal up the structure. Because of him, what is left of the Squaw Island lighthouse will be much more protected from the elements until such time as a complete restoration can take place.

The island is private property that, at this time, cannot be visited.

SKILLAGALEE ISLAND (ILE AUX GALETS) LIGHT | 26

Ile Aux Galets is a narrow strip of land in Lake Michigan about 12 miles northwest of Cross Village that is just large enough to hold a lighthouse. Skillagalee's octagonal, white brick tower, capped in black cast iron, is almost as tall as the island is long. Originally constructed in 1850 and rebuilt several times, this light was automated in the 1960s, and all buildings except for the tower were torn down at that time.

The unassuming island is composed mainly of small pebbles, and fingers of the stones stretch out into the water and slowly disappear beneath the surface. Even from a boat 100 yards from shore, you can peer down into the turquoise depths of Lake Michigan and see the rocky bottom several feet below.

Ile Aux Galets is so low-lying that it seems as though during times of rough water, waves would wash over the entire island and sweep away everything in their path. But a station has stood here for over 140 years, which testifies to its hidden strength. A few shrubs and large trees dot the land near the tower. But except for the stirring of their emerald leaves and flocks of birds that converge on this secluded piece of dry land, hardly anything else moves. For anyone stationed here, gazing at the distant, hazy shoreline of the mainland, this must have been a very lonely post.

LANSING SHOAL LIGHT | 25

The Lansing Shoal Light, built in 1928 about nine miles north of Beaver Island, has a very solid and practical character. Sitting on a large, square concrete foundation, the main floor is a squat, gray metal building trimmed in a darker gray. Windows, covered with what appear to be metal shutters, surround the building, and a short railing lines its roof. Topping the structure is a square tower that rises from the center, its lantern encircled by diamond-paned windows.

27 GRAY'S REEF LIGHT STATION

Built in 1936, Gray's Reef Light Station replaced the last in a series of lightships that had been anchored in the area for 45 years. From its waters, about 23 miles southwest of the Straits, you can see White Shoal, Waugoshance and Skillagalee lights, telling signs of what a hazardous area this is for ships.

Gray's Reef was a difficult light station to build. Construction, which was hampered by dangerous storms and the distance of the project from shore, took two years to complete. The crib structure, for instance, was built in St. Ignace, and then towed the more than 20 miles out to the site. The concrete base includes a rare feature — a steel door near the water line that can be opened from the deck of a visiting ship for easy loading and unloading. A ladder was also built into the concrete base, and a crane on the platform above assists in hoisting materials and supplies. The white structure is encased in steel, and at the second level is a large door, above which spelled out in riveted steel letters is "Grays Reef."

At the top of the two-story base, a fence runs along the perimeter, and at the center the tower narrows considerably in a quick but graceful curve inward. Narrow windows occasionally slit the octagonal tower as it rises to a black parapet and lantern room. Stretching even farther above is a radio tower, its narrow finger piercing the sky high above the water.

Today, this station is not manned, except once each summer when the Coast Guard uses it to monitor the vessels participating in the Chicago to Mackinac Yacht Race.

WHITE SHOAL LIGHT 28

White Shoal Light, 20 miles west of the Mackinac Bridge, is one of the most distinctive lights on Lake Michigan. The structure's concrete base is topped by a low fence border, composed of chains draped lazily from pole to pole. Two cranes still stand near the base of the light, and a narrow band of windows peers out from just above the square, red base of the tower.

This light's most unusual feature is its unique paint job. In 1990 when workers repainted the structure, they again wrapped the tower in red-and-white candy-cane spirals that lead the eye up to the parapet, which is also red. The lantern room no longer houses the original Second Order Fresnel lens, which is now on exhibit at the Whitefish Point Museum.

When this light was built, in 1910, it replaced a lightship that had marked the shoal since 1891. Lightships were vessels that were equipped with lights and other distinctive markings to assist in navigation in areas at one time considered too hazardous to construct permanent lights. Several navigational dangers in this area made it necessary to build additional lights nearby, including Gray's Reef, Waugoshance and Skillagalee.

29 WAUGOSHANCE SHOAL LIGHT

WAUGOSHANCE SHOAL LIGHT

This area near the Straits has always posed a grave hazard for navigators. Beginning in 1832 the dangerous shoal beneath the waves was marked by a lightship anchored on this spot, and it wasn't until 1851 that the Waugoshance Light became the first permanent structure. Many of the materials were assembled on the nearby island of St. Helena then towed out to the site. During one of many reconstructions, monstrous stones were shaped to form huge blocks for the base of the structure. When you look closely at those old, rugged stones, you can still see drilling marks where stabilizing rods were shoved through the rock.

The light was abandoned in 1912 but still stands, even after being used for target practice during World War II. It is clear, though, that it will not survive too many more winters of crushing ice. In its earliest days, the entire structure, from its tower down to the keeper's quarters at its base, was encased in steel to protect it from the elements. All of the tower's steel sheathing, however, has fallen into the blue depths of the lake, exposing the original stone, which seems much too delicate to last for any length of time. The tower is capped by the black "bird cage" skeleton of what used to be the lantern room and parapet.

Everything speaks of decay, from the empty lantern, which used to light up the evening sky with warnings to nearby ships, to the steel walls of the gutted keeper's dwelling at the base. Even the stones at the water's edge seem to be on the verge of collapse, as though — after 100 years — they have neither the strength nor the inclination to carry their load any longer.

OLD MACKINAC POINT LIGHTHOUSE

OLD MACKINAC POINT LIGHTHOUSE 31

In 1957 when Michigan opened its most famous landmark, the Mackinac Bridge, the services of the Old Mackinac Point Lighthouse, in Mackinaw City, were no longer needed. Navigators began using the bridge lights for reference, so the beautiful, old lighthouse was retired and the area surrounding it turned into an equally beautiful park, now open to the public.

The lighthouse was originally built to increase the range of lights in the area, since navigators approaching from the east could not see McGulpin's Point Light. First, in 1890 a fog signal was constructed, then two years later the light began shining across the Straits.

Both the lighthouse and the attached tower are constructed of light-brown brick, and each rests on a tall, solid foundation of gray, rough-cut stones. The circular tower is three stories high, with an interesting decorative pattern of raised brickwork near the top. Several vertical rows of brick, which run down the tower's sides, frame small, round windows just under the walkway. A black cast iron fence tops the tower, and the white lantern is capped by a unique red-tiled roof. The keeper's dwelling is also protected by the beautiful tile, which brilliantly reflects sunlight. White wood braces support small roof overhangs above the entryways, and the large front porch overhang is supported by white columns.

Probably the house's most unusual feature is the large, square two-story tower that forms most of the northern half of the building. Its square-toothed top gives it the appearance of a medieval fortress. Two rows of paired windows rise up the side of this second tower. The exterior trim around all of the windows is painted white, and overall, the tan, white and red colors make this a very visually appealing structure.

Several years ago, this lighthouse complex was fenced in, and an admission fee was charged to enter. But the fence is gone, and today the entire area is a public park, with ample picnic tables. This is a great spot to enjoy a later dinner, take a walk along the Straits of Mackinac's rocky shoreline, then join others who line the water at twilight to watch the beautiful sunsets and the twinkling lights of the Mackinac Bridge.

Mackinaw City is designated as the site of a new Great Lakes Lighthouse Museum, which will be situated on the Old State Ferry Dock on South Huron Street. The museum organization is looking for new members to help with the very exciting work of bringing this monumental project to fruition. Anyone who would like to take part in this unique opportunity should contact the Great Lakes Lighthouse Museum by writing P.O. Box 39, Mackinaw City, MI 49701, or phoning (231) 436-3333.

DIRECTIONS: From I-75 south of Mackinaw City, take exit 336 (Nicolet Ave.). Turn north onto Mackinaw Hwy., which changes to Nicolet Ave. at the city limits, and go approximately 2 miles to its end at Huron Ave. and the entrance to Fort Michilimackinac. You can park either in this area or turn right (east) onto Huron Ave. and go 1½ blocks to the lighthouse parking area, on the left (north).

Note: If you're headed north and miss exit 336, take exit 339, the last exit before crossing the Mackinac Bridge. Turn left (north) onto Nicolet and go 3 blocks to Huron Ave. and the park entrance.

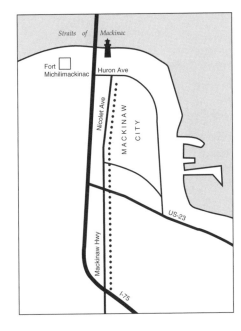

30 McGULPIN'S POINT LIGHTHOUSE

The lighthouse at McGulpin's Point is now a private residence and is not open to the public. Because the lantern room has been removed, it is also no longer visible from the lake.

32 ST. HELENA ISLAND LIGHTHOUSE

One mile from the Upper Peninsula shoreline near the Straits of Mackinac lies the beautiful island of St. Helena. For well over three centuries, native Americans, fur traders, and countless others in small vessels have all taken refuge in the natural harbor on the island's north side. The first group of permanent residents were fishermen and their families, who built homes in the 1830s, and by the time the first lighthouse was established, in 1873, a prosperous town stood on the north shore. Everyone, including the many visitors who briefly went ashore during refueling stops by steamships, was charmed by the simplicity and beauty of the island.

Contact was not limited to the summer months. When the lake froze between the island and Gros Cap, a small settlement on the mainland shore, the island also welcomed visitors. On holidays and other special occasions during the late-19th and early 20th centuries, party-goers could take a three-hour sleigh ride from St. Ignace overland to Gros Cap then out to the island. Crossing the two-mile span of ice however, wasn't necessarily always simple or routine. In 1913 the lighthouse keeper had to rescue two men who had lost their way while attempting the trip.

In 1923 — only 50 years after it had been built on the south shore of the island near a sand bar that stretched out into the water — the lighthouse was automated and its buildings practically abandoned.

Then in 1986 the Great Lakes Lighthouse Keepers Association, a private organization made up of some 1,700 individuals dedicated to the preservation of lighthouses, took an unusual and wonderful step. They obtained a lease to the lighthouse property and began the formi-

dable task of restoring the St. Helena Light.

Time had not been kind to the tower and keeper's dwelling. Holes pockmarked the roof, fire had damaged the second floor, and chunks of fallen plaster littered the floors. Making the repairs even tougher was the fact that all materials and work crews had to be taken by boat to the island.

The association decided that it couldn't handle the huge undertaking in a timely fashion without help. So GLLKA members approached Boy Scout organizations in their areas, and troops 4 and 61 in Ann Arbor and 200 of Calumet/Laurium quickly agreed to play a major role in the restoration. Every summer since 1989, the scouts and GLLKA volunteers have spent hundreds of man-hours helping to restore the structure, even including such details as erecting bird houses and a bat house. Four scouts attained the rank of Eagle Scout, in part by developing projects associated with the saving of the lighthouse.

The vessel that continues to ferry materials and workers to and from the light, the *Cake & Ice Cream,* is also available for charter. Captain Mark Siegman, who also serves as assistant scoutmaster for Troop 323 out of Freeland, will take groups to visit area lights or even scuba dive in the Straits. For details write to Mark at 889 Sanford Road, Midland, MI 48642 or call him at (517) 687-5417 or (906) 643-7937 in St. Ignace on weekends. Proceeds from the charters are used to defray the costs of running this work boat that has helped so much with the St. Helena restoration project.

Today, the two-story red-brown-brick

house stands with pride on its tall stone foundation. White stone supports the main-floor and second-level windows, and small basement windows peep out from below. The exterior of the connected tower is a well-worn white, and the red lantern room stares down from its lofty perch.

From the top of the tower, you can see the island's diverse topography spread out below. The rocky shoreline moves inland to the various greens of wetlands and meadows. Blue herons, osprey and plovers all have found home in the forest and along the shore.

It's wonderfully refreshing to see something this lovely being saved for future generations, not because of the profits it may bring, but because of the joy it will give.

ST. HELENA ISLAND LIGHTHOUSE

33 SEUL CHOIX POINT LIGHTHOUSE

During the mid-1800s Seul Choix Point was the center of a thriving fishing community, but today, only the lighthouse complex is still active. The light still operates, but with an automated replacement for its original Third Order Fresnel lens.

Built between 1892 and 1895, the tower and keeper's dwelling are both set on large, gray stone foundations. The two-story house — easily large enough to accommodate two families — is finished in red brick, including several rooms that have been added on to the original structure. Matching brick archways support the roof of a porch that is deeply recessed into the front of the house. White trim around the windows and eaves contrasts with the deep color of the bricks.

Attached to the house by a small, enclosed corridor of red brick is the nearly 80-foot-tall conical tower. Its white brick exterior has been freshly painted. Small windows are staggered around and up the sides of the tower as they follow the winding stairway inside. Four arched windows are set into stone just below the walkway, whose black trim is matched on its supports as well as on the parapet above.

The lighthouse grounds are well-maintained, with long expanses of grass stretching out to meet the neatly trimmed cedars and pines that dot the lawn. An old wood dryer for fish nets has retired to near the house. And an antique street lamp, the rungs lining its sides still intact, stands waiting for a keeper to climb up and refuel it.

All of the original outbuildings are also still standing, including two oil buildings and a fog signal building.

Since the mid-1970s the Gulliver Historical Society has worked tirelessly to re-create the original beauty of the lighthouse complex through extensive renovations. The main house has been refurnished throughout with original pieces from the early 1900s and also houses a museum and gift shop. New to the museum in 1996 is an exhibit — including a beautiful scale model of the lighthouse — built by Carl Holbrook using over 22,000 hand-cut bricks.

The fog signal building is home to a local history museum and is handicapped accessible. You can tour the complex from mid-June through mid-September, seven days a week, 12 to 4 p.m., depending on the availability of volunteer tour guides. For more information write to the Gulliver Historical Society, RR#1, Box 1, Gulliver, Michigan 49840.

Other facilities at the complex include large picnic areas, restrooms and barbeque pits.

A short trail leads to the shore, and after you walk it, you'll quickly understand the need for this lighthouse. A huge limestone shoal stretches out from beneath your feet and slices through the clear water to nearly 100 yards out from shore. There, waves begin to break, their white foam outlining the shallowest parts of the reef. The shoal plus the land mass of the point itself, which slopes down into the waters of Lake Michigan for nearly three miles, adds up to a very dangerous area for navigators.

Along the beach, tall grasses compete for space between stones and pebbles, and large rocks thrust up out of the water close to shore. Large pines and cedars border the beach, and peeking out through a gap between them is the top of the tower that is beginning its second century of service.

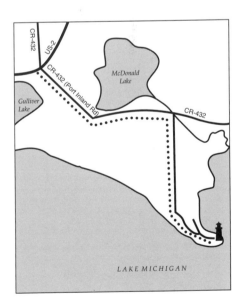

DIRECTIONS: From the junction of US-2 and County Rd. 432 in Gulliver, about 11 miles east of Manistique, go south on CR-432 (Port Inland Rd.) about 4 miles to County Rd. 431. Turn right (west) onto CR-431, which is a gravel road, and go approximately 4 miles to the lighthouse.

Note: When you leave, don't be tempted to turn east onto CR-432. It deadends at the Port Inland Quarry.

34 MANISTIQUE EAST BREAKWATER LIGHT

Not far from shore, at the end of a pier that juts out into Lake Michigan, stands the Manistique East Breakwater Light. The light is housed in a bright-red, square tower that is capped by a black parapet and lantern room. A black staircase climbs up from the pier several feet to the door at the bottom of the tower. Only a few small, round windows allow light into the interior of this structure.

At a lovely park at the shore end of the pier, you can swim and picnic.

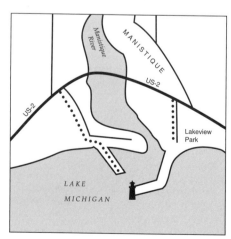

DIRECTIONS: From US-2 near the east city limits of Manistique, turn into Lakeview Park, which borders the highway on the south. This is the easiest place to park, especially if you have an RV or travel trailer, and it's just a short walk along the beach west to the pier and lighthouse.

If you are driving a car, you can also go about 0.3 miles west of Lakeview Park and turn south onto an unmarked road that ends at a cemented parking area and beach near the start of the lighthouse pier.

You can also turn south from US-2 onto the first road west of the bridge over the Manistique River. Go about 2 blocks, just past the entrance to the wastewater treatment plant on the left. Park on the right-hand side of the road and follow one of the short trails that lead through the woods to the lakeshore. In that area is another pier, from which you can get good views and pictures of the pierhead light across the bay.

POVERTY ISLAND LIGHTHOUSE 35

Poverty Island, which lies in Lake Michigan 27 miles southeast of Escanaba, is one in a chain of islands — stretching from Wisconsin's Door Peninsula to Michigan's Garden Peninsula — that mark the entrance to Green Bay.

Most of Poverty Island is bordered by beautiful limestone cliffs, which create a natural breakwater between the powerful waves and the forest 20 feet above. Near the lighthouse, however, the cliffs fade to a shoreline of large rocks dropped in all directions by the powers of nature. fingers of smaller stones stretch out from shore a dozen feet before disappearing beneath the green waters.

The lighthouse sits back about 100 feet from the south shore in a small rocky clearing. The keeper's dwelling and other buildings on the site have been long abandoned, and the white paint of the conical brick tower has nearly worn away. The tower has also suffered the ultimate humiliation of having its lantern removed, leaving an awkward silhouette against the sky, with an empty walkway encircling nothing. A small light, powered by a solar panel has been attached to a pole at the top of the tower.

Despite the abundance of shorebirds in the area, this is a wonderful escape for anyone seeking the solitude and natural beauty of a secluded island. When we visited, campers had pitched their tents near the lighthouse.

36 ST. MARTIN ISLAND LIGHT

St. Martin's Island is located in Lake Michigan nearly halfway between the tip of Michigan's Garden Peninsula and Wisconsin's Door Peninsula. Most of the near-200-acre island is bordered by beautiful, towering cliffs, some over 20 feet high, which match the strength of the waves and shelter the trees that cling to the top of the bluff. Closer to the lighthouse, on the east shore, the cliffs gradually change to a rocky beach, with pebbles piled in mounds by the lake's pounding waters.

Still maintained by the Coast Guard, the tower and dwellings are in very good shape, although the buildings have had their windows boarded up as protection from the elements. Mature cedars dot the surrounding lawn, which is crowded by a thick forest waiting for its chance to move in again. The six-sided steel tower is very narrow, with only a few small, round windows that peer out from beneath the walkway. The walkway, lantern room and roof are all painted black and still enclose a working light, which helps area navigators mark a course.

PENINSULA POINT LIGHT 37

Peninsula Point Light rests at the tip of the strip of land that divides Big Bay de Noc from Little Bay de Noc. In the mid-1800s the newly opened Upper Peninsula iron mines increased Great Lakes traffic in this area to the point that a light here was desperately needed. In 1865 the Peninsula Point

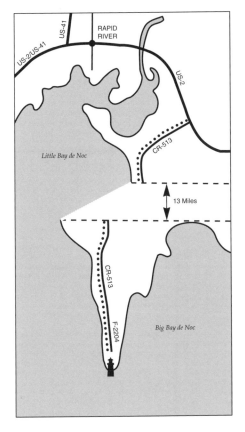

DIRECTIONS: From the junction of US-2 and County Rd. 513, about 3 miles east of Rapid River, turn south onto CR-513 and go about 17.5 miles. As you near the lighthouse, the road changes to F-2204, and for the last mile becomes only one lane with turnouts. If you have a large RV, park it in an RV parking area, on the left at the start of the narrow road. If you are towing a trailer you can unhook it, leave it at the RV area, and drive to the light. Or you can park both vehicle and trailer in the RV area and walk the ¼ mile along the beach or road to the lighthouse.

Light was put into service. The square brick tower was attached to the keeper's house, which was razed by fire in 1959. Fortunately, the tower was saved, and today it is open to the public.

When you look at the isolated tower overlooking the peaceful bay from the center of a large, cleared area, it's hard to imagine that this light station was once filled with activity. In 1888 Jim Armstrong, then a captain in the lighthouse service, brought his family to this remote outpost. His wife, having a small baby to take care of, was a bit put off by what she found. The dwelling was in a state of disrepair, and the previous keeper had even tried his hand at raising chickens in the upstairs bedroom. But not even that was enough to deter them from their duty. They stayed on at the lighthouse for more than 40 years, and their six children were all raised there.

As you would suspect, living in a lighthouse is much different than living in an ordinary dwelling. For instance, once a year, sometimes more often, a lighthouse service inspector would show up at the Armstrong home to check it for perfect cleanliness and orderliness. The Armstrongs, in turn, looked over their children's rooms each morning, and the youngsters often had their own duties to perform, such as helping their father polish the large brass clockwork that ran the light. But they also had many free hours to explore the countryside and shoreline, and as many children who have grown up around lighthouses will tell you, it was the best childhood they could have imagined.

Today, the playful voices of the Armstrongs and others who lived at the light have long since vanished. The empty

lantern overlooks what is now a beautiful picnic area that is part of the Hiawatha National Forest. You can walk in the footsteps of past residents along a 1½-mile interpretive trail, which points out fossils and ancient lake levels as it follows the shoreline.

You can also climb up the 40-foot-tall tower for an impressive view of the bays to the east and west. Visible farther out in the sparkling waters to the south is the Minneapolis Shoal Light. When that light began operating, in 1936, the Peninsula Point Light was no longer needed and was closed.

38 SAND POINT LIGHTHOUSE

The Sand Point Lighthouse at Escanaba is a marvel of renovation. Its Fourth Order lens first illuminated the waters off the point in 1868, and since then its structure has seen several major changes, both inside and out. The first was in 1886, a tragic year for the lighthouse. Fire ravaged the dwelling and also killed its keeper of 18 years, Mary Terry. The building was repaired and used for another 53 years, at which time the Coast Guard shut down the light and remodeled the house into a private dwelling for its personnel. In time the structure was not even recognizable as a lighthouse.

But in the 1980s the Delta County Historical Society obtained a long-term

lease from the Coast Guard and, determined to reclaim a part of their past, its members set out on the Herculean task of returning the structure to its original design. Using century-old blueprints as a guide, they lowered the roof down to its original level, resting on the brick walls. They added a missing 10 feet to the top of the adjoining square brick tower, and they bricked in windows that had not been a part of the original house. Then they stripped and refinished walls and woodwork, and completed other general repairs.

Finally, they took on the daunting task of finding, then obtaining, replacements for the missing parapet and lantern. Their intense search located an old lantern room on Poverty Island, which apparently had been tossed to the ground when it was removed from its tower. That structure and a Fresnel lens, found in Menominee, were brought to Sand Point and put in place.

With justifiable pride the Delta County Historical Society opened the lighthouse, complete with a museum, in July 1990. The building now stands as a reminder to any community of what can be done when pride, determination and conviction become part of your vocabulary.

The lighthouse is located in Ludington Park, which offers a beautiful, sandy beach with a lifeguard and changing rooms.

Also, from the shore here you can see the Escanaba Harbor Light, in the waters about a quarter mile offshore just east of the lighthouse. Built in 1938, the square, white metal tower, with four small portholes peering out from the first two stories, stands on a circular platform lined

with metal siding. The third story is narrower, and a small railing around the top encircles the beacon, which guides ships entering the harbor.

The lighthouse museum is open Memorial Day through Labor Day, seven days a week, 1 p.m. to 9 p.m. For offseason tours write Sand Point Lighthouse, P.O. Box 1776, Escanaba, MI 49829 or call (906) 786-3763.

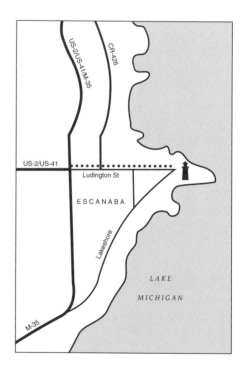

DIRECTIONS: In Escanaba at the junction of US-2/US-41 and M-35, go east on Ludington St., under the arch crossing the road, approximately 1.7 miles to the lighthouse. Immediately behind the lighthouse is the U.S. Coast Guard station and behind it is the Delta County Historical Museum.

MINNEAPOLIS SHOAL LIGHT 39

Though built in the mid-1930s, the Minneapolis Shoal Light, about 10 miles south of Peninsula Point, shows very few signs of age. The only marks from the assault of time are streaks of rust that course down the sides of the cement platform and touch just a few corners of the white tower.

Close to the water line, an iron door and a built-in ladder next to it are still used by Coast Guard personnel, who maintain the light. A white fence borders the top of the solid, square foundation.

The light tower rises from the center of that platform. The first level is a single-story square building, trimmed in bright green from its central door, with two round windows on either side, up to the heavy steel railing that runs along the edge of its roof. Atop this flat structure, the square, white steel tower, bisected with a green stripe, rises four more stories. Gently narrowing from its base, its slender silhouette is broken only by two narrow, square windows on each side. The square, black parapet helps support both the diamond-paned lantern and a small radio tower above the roof of the lantern room.

You can see this light from the mainland, from the tower of the Peninsula Point Light, 10 miles to the north.

CEDAR RIVER LIGHT 40

This lighthouse, about 200 feet back from Lake Michigan at the village of Cedar River, is now a private residence. You can see it, however, from the road adjacent to the lighthouse.

41 MENOMINEE NORTH PIER LIGHT

Sitting at the end of a pier that juts out into Lake Michigan is the Menominee North Pier Light, which has guided boats to the Menominee River since 1877. The current tower, built in the 1920s, rests on a square concrete base painted white, including the steel access doors. The red, 25-foot-high, octagonal tower is topped with a black parapet and lantern room covered by a matching roof. A small door on the tower's shore side at one time opened to a catwalk, which has been removed.

DIRECTIONS: If you enter Menominee from the north on US-41 (10th St.), continue to 10th Ave. and turn left (east). If you enter Menominee from the south on US-41, the highway will turn right (east) onto 10th Ave. Either way, once you are on 10th Ave. continue east until you reach 1st St. Turn right (south) onto 1st and go approximately 0.8 miles to Harbor Dr. Turn left (east) onto Harbor Dr. and follow it to the parking area near the pier and light. This is the same route, marked by signs, that leads to the Menominee River Public Access site.

ONTONAGON LIGHTHOUSE 42

The Ontonagon Lighthouse has been rescued from obscurity by the Ontonagon County Historical Society and the Coast Guard Auxiliary of Ontonagon, which began using the building for meetings in 1969.

Constructed of light-brown brick, the keeper's dwelling is a large two-story structure with dormer windows that poke out of the roof above the second story. The attached square tower, constructed of matching brick, has an outside entry door, with two rectangular windows directly above. The black cast-iron parapet surrounds the octagonal lantern room, which is capped by a black roof. The lightkeeper, here, had the luxury of being able to reach the tower from the inside, not only from the first, but also the second floor of the dwelling.

Because the lighthouse is surrounded by private property, with no official access road, it is not open to the public. You can, however, view it from a parking area across the river (see DIRECTIONS).

Or even better, it's sometimes possible to get a guided tour. Stop in at the Ontonagon County Historical Museum, at 422 River Street (see DIRECTIONS), and they will try to get an escort from the U.S. Coast Guard Auxiliary to escort you to the lighthouse and also give you a tour of the inside, which is in very good condition. The historical museum is usually open from Memorial Day to October 15, seven days a week from 9 a.m. to 5 p.m. However, because the museum is run entirely by volunteers, it's best to call ahead at (906) 884-6165. We were taken to the lighthouse and given a very infor-

mative guided tour by Pat Simons, whose great-grandfather, Thomas Stripe, was keeper of the light from 1864 to 1883.

At the museum itself, you can see the Ontonagon Light's original Fifth Order lens, which was taken from the area in the 1960s and finally returned after years of struggle.

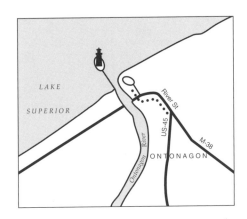

DIRECTIONS: From the junction of US-45 and M-38 in downtown Ontonagon, follow River St. northwest toward the harbor area approximately 0.4 miles. Where the main road turns left (southwest) onto Ontonagon St./M-64 to cross the Ontonagon River, continue straight and look for a parking area ahead and to the left, next to the river. From there you can view the lighthouse across the river.

The Ontonagon County Historical Museum is on the southwest side of River St. about 3 blocks northwest of the US-45/M-38 junction.

43 14 MILE POINT LIGHTHOUSE

Fourteen Mile Point Lighthouse, which once surveyed the waters northeast of the Ontonagon River with pride, has been reduced to a burned-out shell by vandals. From a distance the lighthouse is still a commanding presence on the shoreline, and it is only up close that blue sky peeking through empty windows reveals the indignities this historical structure has suffered.

All of the light's natural beauty, however, has not been extinguished. The red brick walls of the home still rise two stories, and the large, square attached tower continues upward another 20 feet. And glimpses of remnants such as a beautifully tiled floor or a cast iron stove are brief reminders of the vibrant life this lighthouse once had.

The lighthouse is now privately owned and can best be viewed from the water. However, limited tours of the lighthouse are planned after the year 2000. For information write to Keweenaw Video Productions, P.O. Box 665, Houghton, MI 49931.

44 KEEWENAW WATERWAY UPPER ENTRANCE LIGHT

McLain State Park, west of Calumet, takes in more than two miles of beautiful, rugged Lake Superior coastline.

At the southwest corner of the park, a rocky pier stretches out from shore, and off its end stands the Keweenaw Waterway Upper Entrance Light, which guides ships into the Ke-weenaw Waterway, a shortcut across the Keweenaw Peninsula. Its red, steel-covered concrete foundation, surrounded by the blue waters of the lake, supports a square, white building topped on its edges by a black railing. In a few spots, paint has worn from the smooth metal sides to expose the gray undercoating.

Stretching upward from that building is the tower, which begins with a large, square base, then narrows sharply to a slender, still-square tower with round windows peering out from each side. A black guardrail surrounds the exposed

light at the top, and the entire structure stands like a blaze of red and white against the deep-blue waters of Lake Superior.

Farther out from shore, a stone breakwater tames crashing waves, and the-calmer waters behind the wall gently wash up onto the park's sandy beach.

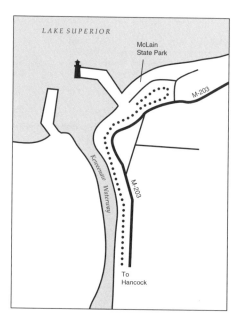

DIRECTIONS: From the junction of US-41 and M-203 in Hancock, follow M-203 and state park signs approximately 10 miles north to the entrance of F.J. McLain State Park. After entering (a daily or annual vehicle pass is required), bear left to reach the lighthouse.

46 EAGLE RIVER LIGHTHOUSE

This lighthouse is now a private residence. Also, unfortunately the view of this light from the water is obscured by a condominium, but you can see it from the main street in Eagle River.

SAND HILLS LIGHTHOUSE 45

Beautiful Sand Hills Lighthouse (also known as 5 Mile Point Lighthouse), about four miles southwest of Eagle River, is an imposing cream-colored brick structure resting on a small rise overlooking Lake Superior. A wide expanse of lawn, broken here and there by clumps of white birch and cedar, stretches down to the water's edge, where waves wash over a stony beach.

A light was needed here to warn of the dangerous Eagle River shoals. The Eagle River light, which was supposed to have served that purpose, was discontinued in 1908 because it was too far inland. In 1917 a temporary light was erected at Sand Hills while the present-day structure was being built. The new lighthouse was the twin of the Scotch Cap Lighthouse on Alaska's Unimac Island. That light, unfortunately, was destroyed by a tidal wave.

The huge Sand Hills Lighthouse, completed in 1919, rises two full stories, with a row of small windows peeking out from a small third level. The front center of the dwelling protrudes, with two separate wings extending back from its sides. The unique design was intended as three separate living quarters for lightkeepers and their families, complete with private front porches overlooking the azure lake below, and a pair of balconies at each corner.

The square tower rises from the center dwelling, and its rectangular windows match those of the house below. The tower is capped by a graceful black lantern room, its crosshatched panes of glass giving it a lovely silhouette.

The only head lightkeeper at this station, which also includes a fog signal building, was William Richard Bennetts, who resided here from 1919 until 1939, when the light was automated. In 1954 the light was officially extinguished.

Recently this impressive light was turned into a bed and breakfast, and guests have a rare opportunity to step into the world of a lightkeeper in the early 1900s. Each room is filled with antique furnishings, a collection that took the owners more than 30 years to accumulate. One of the inn's showpieces is the beautifully restored central staircase, which demonstrates the time and love invested in the renovation of the large building. From the restored English paneling in the living room to the beautiful artwork decorating the home, the Sand Hills Lighthouse Inn is a true gem along the coast of Michigan's Keweenaw Peninsula.

For reservations, call (906) 337-1744 or write to Sand Hills Lighthouse, 5 Mile Point Road, P.O. Box 414, Ahmeek, MI 49901.

The lighthouse is open to the public, with tours May through October between 1 and 4 p.m. conducted for a small fee.

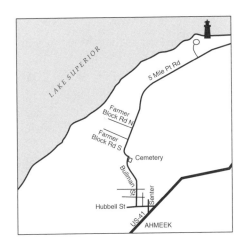

DIRECTIONS: From US-41 in Ahmeek turn north onto Senter St. (a sign at this junction reads "Five Mile Point 8 miles / Eagle River 12 miles.") and go one block to Hubbell St. Turn left (west) onto Hubbell and go 2 blocks To Bellman St. Turn right (north) onto Bellman and drive approximately 7.8 Miles to the 5 Mile Point Lighthouse, on the left. (As Bellman leaves Ahmeek and passes a cemetery on the right, it becomes 5 Mile Point Rd.)

47 EAGLE HARBOR LIGHTHOUSE

The first lighthouse at Eagle Harbor was built in 1851, and the station has undergone many changes in the last 140 years, including a new tower, erected in 1871, and a fog signal, added in 1895. In 1912 a life saving station began operation across the harbor from the lighthouse. As was often the case, the station and the lighthouse compound shared common management and a common goal — the safety of travelers on the lake.

One of the most-trying episodes in the life saving station's history began during a late November storm in 1926. The men at the station were notified that a ship, the *Thomas Maytham*, was hung up on rocks some 40 miles away. Immediately, the rescue crew set off in their motorized boat and, after braving below-zero temperatures and towering waves, reached the ship and took on its 22 crew members.

But instead of making the six-mile trip to the Mendota Light Station, they decided — for reasons they never could explain — to make the much longer return trip to their own station at Eagle Harbor, even though the storm was worsening.

It was a fateful decision. On the return trip, the lifesaving crews spotted an ice- and snow-covered shape that they barely recognized as another ship, the *Bangor*, which had run hard aground. Its crew had made it to shore but were in grave danger of suffering from exposure. After dropping off the men of the *Maytham*, the station's crew returned in their boat to rescue the 29 people of the *Bangor*.

A white building, which was originally part of that Coast Guard life saving station, was later moved across the harbor to behind the lighthouse, where today it is in use as a dwelling. And the lighthouse, itself, is still the area's most prominent landmark, welcoming visitors from both land and lake.

The lighthouse sits on the tip of a narrow promontory of rock that marks the western entrance to the harbor. Large rocks angle out in front of the tower until they are finally submerged beneath the icy waters of Lake Superior. A few trees cling to the shoreline in front of the house, but the tower stretches far above their green leaves.

The beautiful two-story house is sided with red brick, and window trim and decorative eaves are painted white. The lakeside face of the attached eight-sided red-brick tower has also been painted white, and a white walkway surrounds the lantern room. The structure is topped by a dark-red roof.

The Keweenaw County Historical Society operates a fascinating nautical and historical museum in the lighthouse and surrounding buildings. The museum is open from mid-June through September, seven days a week, noon to 5 p.m.

DIRECTIONS: As you enter Eagle Harbor from the west on M-26, where the highway turns sharply right (south) at the harbor and beach area, do not turn right but rather go left onto a short road that goes up over a small hill and through a gate into the fenced-in lighthouse parking area. If approaching Eagle Harbor from the east on M-26, the highway makes a sharp right-hand turn, briefly runs along the beach area, then makes a sharp turn left (west). At that turn, continue straight and follow the short bayside road to the lighthouse parking area.

ROCK OF AGES LIGHT 48

The Rock of Ages Light — 18 miles from the mainland and 4.5 miles from the shores of Isle Royale — is one of the most remote on the Great Lakes. It was built, in 1908, so that ships could bypass the passage around the southern, more-weather-exposed side of Isle Royale in favor of the safer route along the lee side of the island. Even so, during a heavy fog in 1933, the passenger steamer *George M. Cox* ran aground and its 125 passengers and crew had to be taken into the lighthouse, where they were warmed and fed until they could be moved to the mainland the following day.

In the earliest years of this century, the lighthouse service brought out supplies only to lightships and crib lights. All other lightkeepers were expected to fend for themselves, as best they could, no matter how remote a chunk of land they were stationed on. As a result, the first keepers of Rock of Ages had to travel 54 miles by sailboat to the closest town, Port Arthur, Ontario, to pick up their mail and supplies.

The rock that supports the Rock of Ages light is not only isolated, but also small, stretching perhaps 150 feet at its longest point. the center of this rock was dynamited level to provide a solid foundation for the tower, leaving small outcroppings of rock on either side of the light. One solitary small bush clings to the top of the stone, and orange moss covering the rock's surface is the only other color in the gray surroundings.

The cement foundation for the tower rises from the rock about 15 feet, and a fence encircles the platform on top. At the center, the circular tower rises two stories, smoothly narrows its diameter, then continues upward three more stories.

Several windows dot the tower's smooth, white surface, and the black of the window trim is matched on the parapet, lantern room and roof. A narrow stairway leads down from the cement platform to the top of a section of rock that, in turn, joins a dock stretching out into the water.

When first erected, the 4,500,000 candlepower of its beacon made the Rock of Ages Light the brightest on the Great Lakes. In 1978 this light, following the fate of so many others on the lakes, was automated. A naked flagpole still stands as a reminder of the activity that was

once so integral a part of this light station. The original Second Order Fresnel lens is on display at the Windigo Visitors Center on Isle Royale, and the once-full lantern room now houses a small beacon that needs no help from humans to light itself as darkness falls and extinguish itself at the break of day.

You can see this light from the decks of either of the two ferries that carry visitors to Isle Royale from Grand Portage, Minnesota. For more details see, *Rock Harbor Light*, p. 51)

49 MENAGERIE ISLAND LIGHTHOUSE

Menagerie Island, just off the south shore center of Isle Royale, has a very unusual; rock foundation. The layer of rock has been pushed up above the surface of Lake Superior at a 45-degree angle, in exactly the same way as other rocks that formed the Keweenaw Peninsula, but in the opposite direction. The unusual prehistoric, geologic maneuvers left little room for anything to take root on the small chunk of rock. A tiny clump of bushes that has survived near the center of the island provides the only touch of natural color.

Menagerie Island is an odd name for something so desolate and lifeless. About the closest the place came to being a menagerie was when the 13 children of one lighthouse keeper and his wife overran the small island. Like most children who lived at lighthouses around the Great Lakes, they rarely lacked for something to do. Occasionally, for instance, they would take a small boat out to the surrounding smaller islands and gather the eggs of nesting birds. The family would pickle the eggs back at the lighthouse and then sell the welcome delicacy to the crews of passing ships.

Today, the light has been automated and the island returned to its abandoned state. The octagonal brick tower is losing its bright, white paint, and patches of dark brick are showing through. The black parapet and lantern room no longer provide lonely residents with their first glimpse of welcome visitors. The attached keeper's dwelling is made of reddish-brown brick, and its windows have been boarded up to protect it from the harsh environment. The rocks in front of the light are brushed with a hint of the yellow moss that is so common among

the islands here, and the angled stone swiftly plunges beneath the surface of the sapphire-blue waters of Lake Superior.

You can see this light aboard the *Voyager*, a ferry that carries passengers to Isle Royale from Grand Portage, Minnesota. For more details, see *Rock Harbor Light*, p. 51).

ROCK HARBOR LIGHTHOUSE 50

Rock Harbor Lighthouse rests on the southeast shore of America's least-visited National Park — Isle Royale, in northern Lake Superior 56 miles from the Michigan mainland. Isle Royale is truly one of Michigan's, and the nation's, jewels. It is rugged yet approachable, and its rocky shoreline surrounds a heavily forested wilderness filled with the wonder of wolves and moose.

The Rock Harbor Lighthouse was originally built in 1855, but operated only sporadically until 1879, when the light on Menagerie Island took over the job of illuminating the area. In the early 1960s, more than 30 years after Isle Royale became a national park, the U.S. Park Service began restoring the light and its tower.

A wide, dark stone porch leads to the door of the keeper's single-story dwelling, which is constructed of sturdy, rough stone, as is the attached tower. Both structures are painted white, and the house sports dark wood shutters to protect the windows. The black parapet peers out just above the tree line, and the empty lantern is capped by a rusted dome. In front, pines shadow most of the house and part of the tower. Where the trees stop, yellow mosses begin to crawl toward the water. A low rise of stone meets the powerful waves of the lake, then quietly dives beneath the water.

Though it is possible to visit Isle Royale just for the day, most visitors arrive on government-chartered ferries and stay overnight or longer at Rock Harbor Lodge, in cottages that overlook Tobin Harbor, or at any of several rustic and primitive campgrounds throughout the 210-square-mile wilderness island.

There are three departure ports for Isle Royale — Copper Harbor and Houghton, Michigan, and Grand Portage, Minnesota — and it is possible to see one or more of the area's lights (Rock of Ages, Passage Island, Menagerie Island, and Rock Harbor) on some of the cruises.

From Copper Harbor the *Isle Royale Queen III* sails directly to Rock Harbor Lodge, near the island's northeast end, and does not pass any of the area lighthouses at a close distance.

If you ride the *Ranger III* out of Houghton, you will pass the Rock Harbor Light on your way to the Rock Harbor Lodge.

From the decks of the *Wenonah*, which sails out of Grand Portage, Minnesota, you can see the Rock of Ages Light. The captain, if asked and if possible, will change course for an even closer view of that light before docking at the Windigo Visitors Center, on the southwest end of the island. On display inside, there, is the Second Order Fresnel Lens from the Rock of Ages Light.

The *Voyager,* which also departs out of Grand Portage, makes a stop at the Windigo Visitors Center then rounds the north shore to Rock Harbor Lodge. On that part of the trip, you can see the Passage Island Light from a distance. After an overnight stay in Rock Harbor, the *Voyager* heads southwest and passes the Rock Harbor, Menagerie Island, and Rock of Ages lights before making a brief stop, again at Windigo, then returning to Grand Portage. Upon request and if conditions permit, the captain will swing closer to the Rock of Ages Light. And during the stop at Windigo, there's just enough time to get a look at that light's Second Order Fresnel lens, on display in the visitors center.

While on Isle Royale, itself, you can take regularly scheduled trips to the Passage Island and Rock Harbor lights aboard the tour boat *Sandy.*

You can also see the Rock Harbor Light by renting a boat at Rock Harbor Lodge and rowing about five miles to the old log buildings of the former Edisen Fishery camp. There, a quarter-mile path rises up a gradual incline then drops down the other side to the lighthouse.

For more details about Isle Royale's facilities, transportation and schedules, contact Isle Royale National Park, 87 N. Ripley St., Houghton, MI 49931; (906) 482-0984.

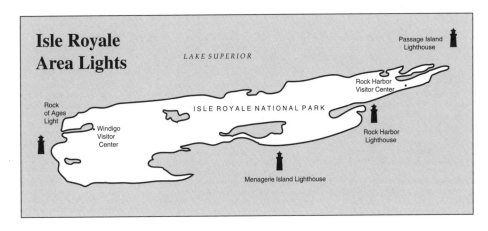

ROCK HARBOR LIGHTHOUSE

PASSAGE ISLAND LIGHTHOUSE 51

The Passage Island Lighthouse marks the point where ships have to pass between this island and Isle Royale, to the south. Its unusual-looking fissured and ridged rock surface is actually quite common among the islands in northern Lake Superior. The tall stone ridges along the shore have been worn smooth by the action of the ancient glaciers, and golden grasses that have filled the hundreds of small, regular cracks in its surface create a cross-hatched pattern in the rock. Beyond the stone boundaries, a pine forest rises up to thickly cover soft, undulating hills at the center of the near-300-acre island.

The lighthouse complex stands at the edge of a sheer rock wall on the north shore of the island. The rocks there have been pushed up at the same angle but to different heights, which makes the shore look slightly off balance. In front of the lighthouse, mosses cling to the smooth stone in a cascade of yellow and orange all the way down to the high-water mark at the shore. The white wood fog whistle building still stands, and modern structures such as a tall, red radio tower and solar panels have been added to the compound.

But all of these additions are forgotten the instant you turn your attention to the 110-year-old lighthouse itself. Both the house and attached tower were built in the same style. The main walls are constructed of varying shades of dark-brown stone, with white mortar outlining their irregular patterns. Around the doors, windows and buttresses of the tower, light-brown cut sandstone has been used to give added support. The symmetry of the sandstone contrasts with the rough, irregularly shaped, darker stone, making a beautifully natural, colorful pattern. The first floor of the tower is square, then it becomes six-sided with only a few small windows trimmed in white. The white parapet circles the empty lantern room, and the entire structure is capped by a red metal roof and ventilator ball.

Although Passage Island is a remote destination, the beauty of its lighthouse is well worth the additional effort it takes to see it. One view comes from the decks of the *Voyager*, a ferry that carries passengers from Grand Portage, Minnesota, to Isle Royale National Park. Or from Isle Royale, itself, you can take a ride to Passage Island aboard the tour boat *Sandy*. For more details, see *Rock Harbor Light*, p. 51.

52 COPPER HARBOR FRONT RANGE & REAR RANGE LIGHTHOUSE

The original Copper Harbor Range light building, built shortly after the Civil War, is now being used as a residence by the assistant manager of Ft. Wilkins State Park. You're welcome to take photographs of the area, but please respect the privacy of the residents.

The first level of the two-story wood-sided house is painted chocolate brown, while the upper level is white with brown trim. Dormer windows extend from the angle of the roof, and a large brick chimney peers over the roof line. A small,

square room that rests on the flattened peak at one end of the roof once housed the original rear range light. The lantern flame shone through a small, arched window at the front of the room. An unusual rectangular platform that juts out from below the window now holds an antenna.

The present-day rear range light is on a steel-skeleton tower about 100 feet in front of the house. Facing the harbor at the top of the structure is a white steel panel with a vertical red line through its center, which creates a bright visual focus

for boats offshore. The top of the tower also supports a small beam, which is directed at the lake beyond.

The old front range light was replaced more than 60 years ago by a new light, located near the water's edge. The new structure is a miniature version of the new rear range, with a similar red-striped white panel topped by the beacon. A square, red steel foundation about five feet tall supports the panel and light.

FRONT RANGE LIGHT

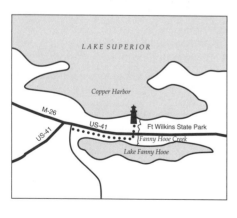

REAR RANGE LIGHTHOUSE

DIRECTIONS: From the junction of US-41 and M-26 on the west side of Copper Harbor, go east approximately one mile to Fanny Hooe Creek. Cross over the creek and turn left into a parking area next to the creek. Although you are on state park land, there is no charge to visit the range lights. If you have a large motor home or trailer, continue down the main road to Fort Wilkins and park in the lot near the fort entrance. It's just a short walk back to Fanny Hooe Creek.

You can view the Front and Rear Range lights back across the creek. Although the lights are on state park property, it is a private residence. You are welcome to take pictures in this area, but please respect it as private property.

COPPER HARBOR LIGHTHOUSE 53

The Copper Harbor Lighthouse is on mainland state-park property, but because there is no public access road, you can only get to it by water via a state-chartered ferry boat. But instead of an inconvenience, the ferry ride is a wonderful opportunity for taking photos or simply enjoying the beauty of Copper Harbor. The 15-minute cruise departs from the Municipal Pier in the town of Copper Harbor and runs the length of the harbor, which is bordered on the north by a chain of small islands. As you approach the lighthouse dock, listen for the gentle ringing of a fog bell anchored a short distance from shore. The soft, rhythmic clang will provide a pleasant backdrop to your entire visit here.

From directly in front of the boat dock, a trail turns to the right, past pines and cedar, which cover most of the area. The path heads to the shoreline, where the rocky terrain slopes toward Lake Superior. Big chunks of rock have fallen from shore to become dark monoliths surrounded by the cold, clear water. Driftwood, lying stranded on the rocky slopes, provides only an echo of life on the inhospitable shore. Placed strategically along the trail are anchors, propellers, and other maritime artifacts recovered from area shipwrecks.

To the left of the boat dock is the original keeper's cottage, a relic of a simpler lifestyle far removed from what most of us are used to. Nestled on the rocky shore, the quaint building is made of area stone, and its wood roof shingles are covered with a thin layer of dark-green moss. A cement path and stairway lead from the cottage to the lighthouse, which is on a small hill overlooking the harbor. Built in 1866, the light-brown brick tower and attached house — with its dark-red roof, small back porch (with its own steeply sloped roof), and crisp-white shutters — form a commanding yet friendly picture. The tower itself is square, with a black iron walkway surrounding the glass-enclosed parapet that has its own red-shingled roof.

This is the second light constructed at this site. The first light tower, now gone, was built in 1849 and stood near the site of a large steel tower that rises directly in front of the present-day lighthouse, The light was taken out of the present-day lighthouse and placed in the steel tower in 1927, after which time the lighthouse was no longer used. Today, it houses a nautical museum on both the first and second floors. You cannot, however, climb past the second floor into the tower.

There was plenty of activity in the area prior to the construction of the first light. Douglass Houghton blasted on a vein of copper at the lakeshore near the lighthouse, and the first commercial copper mine in the Keweenaw Peninsula later worked that deposit. You can still see the mine shaft, now fenced off, on the walking tour.

DIRECTIONS: You can view the Copper Harbor Light from the Lake Superior shore in the area of the Copper Harbor Range Lights.

Boats to the Copper Harbor Light, chartered by the state park, depart from the Municipal Marina, located on the north side of M-26 just west of the turnoff to Brockway Mountain Dr., on the west side of Copper Harbor. The tour boat departs Memorial Day weekend - July 3rd at 10 a.m., 12 noon, and 2 and 4 p.m.; July 4 - August 6, 10 a.m. to 5 p.m. hourly; and August 26 - September 30, 10 a.m., 12 noon, and 2 and 4 p.m. During the tour season you may phone (906) 289-4966 for further details.

LAKE SUPERIOR

Municipal Marina
M-26
Brockway Mt Drive
US-41
Copper Harbor
US-41
Ft Wilkins State Park
Lake Fanny Hooe

54 GULL ROCK LIGHTHOUSE

Gull Rock Lighthouse lies nearly two miles off the tip of the Keweenaw Peninsula, between the mainland and Manitou Island. It is aptly named. Other than the lighthouse itself, the only things in view here are the small area of rock the lighthouse is perched on and the numerous seagulls that call this island home. With barely enough dry land to build on and none of it suitable for any kind of planting, this must have been one of the loneliest assignments a Lake Superior lighthouse keeper would have to endure. The island is so small, in fact, that during stormy weather waves wash over the entire area, leaving only the house and its square brick tower, unprotected and alone, to withstand the force of nature.

Gull Rock is abandoned and closed to the public, but as with nearly all Michigan lighthouses, you can view it from the deck of a boat. Be advised, however, that because of dangerous reefs in the area you should not approach too near the island. And it would be difficult to land any but very small boats on the island itself.

MANITOU ISLAND LIGHT 55

Manitou Island, which lies about 2½ miles east of the tip of the Keweenaw Peninsula, is ringed by a shore of dark-gray stone that plunges beneath the surface of Lake Superior. Directly in front of the lighthouse, a stone wall reinforces the shoreline against erosion by waves and ice. And farther inland, a thick, green forest nearly covers the small, oblong island.

The tower is a narrow four-story steel cylinder topped by the parapet and lantern room. External steel bracing supports the cylinder, which looks barely large enough to enclose a stairway. Dozens of square panes enclose the round lantern room, and the steel cap is now dull red. The keeper's dwelling, a single-story building, adjoins the tower at the back. Other outbuildings still stand nearby, including a large, white single-story structure with its own attached square two-story tower.

56 BETE GRISE LIGHTHOUSE

The Bete Grise, or Mendota, Lighthouse is now a private residence on the shore of the Mendota Ship Canal, which connects Lac LaBelle to Keweenaw Bay. The pale-yellow two-story dwelling is trimmed in dark brown, and the attached small, square tower is also painted yellow. The parapet rises just over the roof line, but its 10-sided lantern room is now empty. Narrow pines and low-lying bushes that border the structure complete the picturesque setting.

You can view the scene from a road across the canal from the lighthouse.

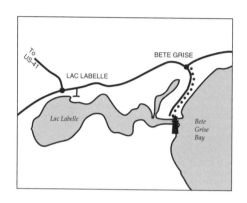

DIRECTIONS: From US-41 approximately one mile east of Delaware, turn south onto the road to Lac LaBelle. Go approximately 4.5 miles to Lac LaBelle, then turn left and follow the main road (turn sharply south at Bete Grise) about 4.5 miles to its end, at the Mendota Ship Canal. From there you can see and get good pictures of the lighthouse, which is across the canal.

57 PORTAGE RIVER LOWER ENTRANCE LIGHT
58 JACOBSVILLE LIGHTHOUSE

The lower entrance light to the Portage River and the Keweenaw Waterway is at the end of a pier that stretches out into Keweenaw Bay. The four-story tower sits on a wide, square concrete base that also holds a foghorn building. The tower — its windows long sealed up and painted over — presents an unbroken face of white. Diamond-shaped windows in the lantern room give the black iron parapet a distinctive appearance, and a red cap gives it color. The pier leading out to the light makes for a lovely walk, and its rounded surface has no fence or railing to mar your view of the beautiful bay surrounding you.

From the pier you can also view the Jacobsville Lighthouse, now a private residence, about ½ mile up the shore to the east.

SAND POINT LIGHTHOUSE 59

The Sand Point lighthouse rests on the shore of beautiful Keweenaw Bay near Baraga. The small 1½-story keeper's house is built of red brick, and a large screened porch runs the length of the home. The square tower rises 40 feet and is topped with a white wooden walkway and octagonal lantern room. Framed by the lacey branches of towering pines behind and a strip of white sandy beach in front, the lighthouse is a charming destination.

The Sand Point lighthouse has recently been purchased by the Keweenaw Bay Indian Community, whose long-term plans call for complete restoration of this historic structure.

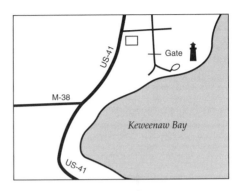

DIRECTIONS: From the intersection of US-41 and M-38 in Baraga, go north on US-41 0.8 mile to an unnamed black top road immediately past the DNR District headquarters. (A sign at this junction reads "Ojibway Campgrounds, Public Welcome.") Turn right (east) onto the unnamed road and go 0.2 mile to a gravel road. Turn right (south) onto the gravel road and go 0.2 mile to where you will pass through a gate. About 50 feet past the gate the road forks; take the left fork and go about 0.2 mile to the Lighthouse. (Note: No one under 17 years old is allowed without a parent).

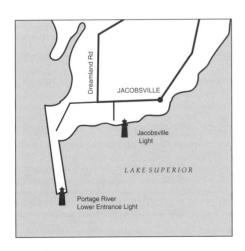

DIRECTIONS: One block south of where M-26 makes a sharp turn on the north edge of Lake Linden, turn east onto the road to Jacobsville. As it leaves town, the road becomes Bootjack Rd. Follow Bootjack, as it turns south around the tip of Torch Lake, about 7 miles to a fork in the road at Dreamland. Take the left fork, Dreamland Rd., about 9 miles to a "T" intersection. turn right (west) onto the gravel road (the road on the left is asphalt), and go about 0.7 miles to its end at a small park near the pier and light.

PORTAGE RIVER LOWER ENTRANCE LIGHT

60 HURON ISLANDS LIGHTHOUSE

The Huron Islands lie about three miles north of the Lake Superior shoreline about midway between Big Bay and L'Anse. These few rocky islands, which take their name from the mountain range on land directly to the south, have some of the most-rugged coastline on Lake Superior.

In 1868 a lighthouse was built on West Huron Island, the largest of the group, to warn mariners of the dangers here. West Huron Island is comprised of softly rounded stone, whose smooth surface has been cracked countless times by the elements. The fissures nearest the lake have caused large sections of rock to break away and tumble into the icy waters. In some areas the fallen rocks left sheer cliffs, while in others the smooth stone angles easily down to the water's edge. The rounded crests of all the islands are covered with a thick growth of hardwoods, but most of the green comes from the narrow spires of pines firmly anchored to even the most inhospitable stone.

The lighthouse was built on the highest crest of West Huron Island, and its stone construction blends with the light-brown rock that covers the summit. Areas of the rock around the lighthouse have cracked into large, square sections, and wild grasses that have brown in the fissures create a checkerboard appearance. The keeper's dwelling, which is trimmed in white, features dormer windows on the second floor. The square tower is attached, and the corners of both the tower and house have all been outlined in white stone, as have the windows and door, which gives the structure a distinctive, very beautiful appearance. The white lantern room still houses a working light.

Another dwelling stands beside the original keeper's house, and near the shore are several other buildings plus a loading dock and a long, narrow staircase that descends the rocky cliff to the shoreline below — all evidence that, at one time, this must have been a bustling light station.

Top left: Livingstone Memorial Light

Top right: White Shoal Light

Bottom: South Manitou Island Light

Menagerie Island Light

South Haven South Pier Light

Big Bay Point Lighthouse

South Fox Island Light

Port Austin Reef Light

BIG BAY POINT LIGHTHOUSE 61

The Big Bay Point Lighthouse, one of only two lighthouses in Michigan that operates as a bed and breakfast inn, is also one of the most beautiful on the Great Lakes. Its view from atop a bluff nearly 100 feet above the timeless waves of Lake Superior is unparalleled. The grounds are understated charm, from the wild rosebushes that spill over a low fence near shore, then cling to the bluff's edge, to the large plantings of tiger lilies that border the house.

The lighthouse, built in 1896, is in excellent condition. The large, immaculate keeper's dwelling is made of red brick with limestone reinforcements at the corners and above the first-floor windows. The attached square tower rises from the north side of the house, and the brickwork near the top resembles the parapet of a medieval castle. A tall railing borders the brick tower, and a smaller octagonal room rises from its center to hold the lantern room and red roof.

A small, automated Coast Guard beacon in the yard nearby is now used as a navigational aid. The light's original Fresnel lens is on display in the old fog whistle building.

Visitors are welcome on the grounds daily from 10 a.m. to 4 p.m., (park at the gate and make the short walk up to the lighthouse), and tours are available May through September on Tuesday, Thursday and Sunday afternoons at 1:00, 1:30 and 2:00 for a cost of $2.00.

For further information write Big Bay Point Lighthouse, #3 Lighthouse Rd., Big Bay, MI 49808, phone (906) 345-9957, or visit their web page at www.LighthouseBandB.com.

Big Bay is a year-round retreat with a variety of opportunities for outdoor adventures, including fishing, mountain biking, and trips to waterfalls. The hiking trails surrounding the lighthouse double as cross-country ski trails in the winter.

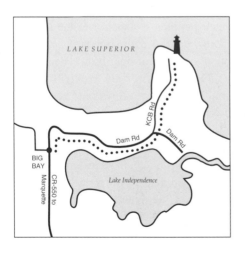

DIRECTIONS: From Wright St. on the north edge of Northern Michigan University in Marquette, turn north onto Sugar Loaf Ave., which turns into County Rd. 550, and go about 25 miles to Big Bay. Follow CR-550 to the north end of Big Bay, then turn right (east) onto Dam Rd. Follow Dam Rd approximately 2 miles to a "T" intersection. Turn left (north) onto KCB (Lighthouse) Rd. and go about a mile to the lighthouse. The Big Bay Lighthouse is a private residence that is run as a bed and breakfast inn.

62 STANNARD ROCK LIGHT

In 1835 the first American-made ship finally began to ply its trade along the Lake Superior shore. It was the *John Jacob Astor,* captained by Charles C. Stannard, who later also was the first to spot the huge rock that is submerged in the middle of the lake. It now bears his name and holds one of the most desolate lights on the Great Lakes.

Stannard Rock, located about 50 miles north of Marquette, is very similar to an underwater mountain. From its "peak," which is only four feet below the surface, very shallow depths — 14 to 20 feet, and in some places less — extend out nearly a quarter of a mile. Since it is near shipping lanes so far from shore, it was a particularly dangerous spot before the light was erected and was sometimes referred to as the "Sailors Graveyard."

Even after the lighthouse was built, danger still threatened. Because of Stannard Rock's location, any approaching storm is able to build up intensity as it travels the length of Lake Superior before slamming into the lighthouse. The keepers knew that they should not take any storm lightly at Stannard Rock.

But one November a maintenance crew found out the hard way. The 12 men had been working on the light for several weeks and were nearing the end of the job when a storm blew up and quickly trapped them inside the light. The hours turned to days, and their home became a prison, as nearly a foot of ice sealed the doors shut Then drift ice began moving in. Predominant winds blew sheets of the pack ice across the length of the lake and hit the lighthouse full force. Gale winds slammed tons of ice against the tower and platform, shaking the stone with every onslaught.

When it was over, the men found themselves trapped by 12 feet of ice. By then they had already spent seven days in the lighthouse, and food was running out. But it took another two days of chopping before the men finally broke through the ice to the outside. They were in no mood to wait for the lighthouse tender to return and pick them up. Instead, they took the small lighthouse boat through the dangerous ice field to the mainland and arrived on welcome shore unharmed.

Even today the treacherous waters of Lake Superior have not been conquered, and we had to cancel several boat trips to the rock because of bad weather or high waves. Finally, we arranged to be flown out. From the air you can see the beautiful design of the reef near the lighthouse. As the rock rises toward the surface, the dark blues of the lake lighten to green, with the palest greens covering the sections closest to the surface.

On the edge of a dropoff, the tower rises from the center of a circular breakwater that, in turn rests on a timber crib reinforced with huge chunks of stone. A small building is attached to the base of the tower, and both structures are made of solid blocks of light-brown stone. The walls of the tower are broken by four small, square windows, and the black parapet and lantern room raise the light to a total of 102 feet above the lake level.

The Stannard Rock tower stands, always prepared, in mute testimony to the fact that no matter how sophisticated our technology, we still cannot stop the dangers of nature. We can only warn each other about them.

GRANITE ISLAND LIGHTHOUSE

Offshore about 11 miles north of Marquette is Granite Island, home to one of the most artistically crafted lighthouses on the lake. Though you can still appreciate the beauty of this light, unfortunately there are reminders that may not be true for long.

The keeper's dwelling and attached square tower are both beautifully constructed of cut stone, with white limestone bordering the corners of the house, tower and all windows. Despite their rugged construction, the structures are beginning to deteriorate. A hole in the roof near the lone dormer window exposes a dark, gaping section, and the long-abandoned fog-bell tower is entirely rusted.

The windows, however, have been boarded up in an attempt to slow down any further damage. And recently, the lighthouse changed from U.S. Coast Guard to private ownership.

The island, itself, is nothing more than a large chunk of granite, with barely enough area to give a few stunted bushes and grasses a foothold. But mosses have found a welcome home here, and their yellows and greens cling firmly to the sheer rock walls. And this perch is also a favorite of gulls.

64 PRESQUE ISLE HARBOR LIGHT

Presque Isle is a beautiful peninsula joined to the mainland at Marquette by a thin strip of land. Extending out into Presque Isle Harbor south from the peninsula's narrow base is a rugged stone breakwater. A wide, octagonal concrete platform at its end holds the Presque Isle Harbor Breakwater Light. The narrow, cylindrical tower is illuminated with a few small portholes, and at its top a red beacon still guides ships into the area.

Presque Isle is a park within the city limits of Marquette, and its variety of attractions makes it a favorite of both local residents and tourists. Near the entrance, you can splash away the afternoon at a water park that includes Shiras Pool, Michigan's largest manmade swimming pool. Closer to the harbor's water, a large expanse of shade-dappled lawn has been set aside as a picnic area. Through the heart of the park, a winding road runs along the shore, which is lined with huge stone bluffs. You can pull off at several lookouts and take in the beauty that comes with being 100 feet above lake level.

On the west side of the isle, near Shiras Pool, the land drops down to near lake level. A lush lawn that stretches from a nearby parking area to the water's edge looks to be a convenient place to picnic.

Also, from a viewing area near the giant Lake Superior and Ishpeming Railroad Ore Dock, just outside the park entrance, you can get close-up looks at huge ore boats being loaded with taconite.

DIRECTIONS: On the south side of Marquette where US-41/M-28 makes a 90-degree bend, go north onto Front St., drive about 6 blocks until you pass under the Soo Line ore trestle, then turn right (east) at the next street, which is Main. Go one block on Main and turn left (north) onto Lakeshore Blvd. Follow Lakeshore as it turns east then north approximately 3¼ miles to Presque Isle City Park.

MARQUETTE HARBOR LIGHTHOUSE

65

The Marquette Harbor Lighthouse is one of the most picturesque on Lake Superior. Resting on an expansive stone bluff, its bright-red sides dominate the horizon, and the adjoining square tower looks powerfully out toward Lake Superior. The lantern room and window trim are both white, but the metal roof and ventilator ball of the tower are painted red. Green bushes border the ground floor of this two-story building, and bits of brush find a difficult foothold along the upper portions of the stony cliff.

This is an active Coast Guard station, and so the lighthouse is not open to visitors. The best photo opportunities therefore are from the beach just north of the lighthouse or from the lower harbor breakwall area.

Marquette is a city very proud of its nautical history, and the Marquette Maritime Museum, at the corner of East Ridge and Lakeshore Drive, is worth a stop for anyone interested in nautical history.

(DIRECTIONS and map, page 66.)

66 MARQUETTE LOWER HARBOR BREAKWATER LIGHT

The Marquette South Breakwater Light rests on a concrete base at the end of a stone pier that extends out into Lake Superior to protect the waters off the shores of Marquette. The light is housed atop a narrow, white cylinder.

Most pier lighthouse designs included a catwalk, so keepers could get to the lights above the waves and ice. But when this light was first built, architects and engineers solved the problem of bad-weather access in an original way. With the construction of the light and breakwater, a tunnel was also built beneath, from shore down the length of the pier to the inside of the light at the end.

In later years the wall was extended but the tunnel was not, and a new light was constructed at the end of the new pier. Because of the danger it presented to would-be explorers, the unused tunnel was eventually sealed up and today is seen only in the memories of a few of the area's long-time residents.

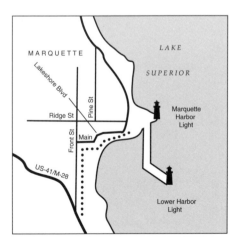

DIRECTIONS: On the south side of Marquette where US-41/M-28 makes a 90-degree bend, go north onto Front St., drive about 6 blocks until you pass under the Soo Line ore trestle, then turn right (east) at the next street, which is Main. Go one block on Main and turn left (north) onto Lakeshore Blvd. As Lakeshore bears right (east), look for a large parking area on the right, at Ellwood Mattson Park. From there you can take a boat tour of the Marquette area that includes from-the-water views of all three Marquette-area lights. For cruise information and schedules, call Marquette Harbor Cruises at (906) 225-1777.

Continue east on Lakeshore Blvd. until it turns left (north). Near that turn you can park and see the Lower Harbor pier and light, and the maritime museum, the U.S. Coast Guard station and the Marquette Harbor Lighthouse. Because this is an active Coast Guard facility, you cannot visit the lighthouse, but you can take pictures.

END OF THE ROAD RANGE LIGHTS

The abandoned front and rear range lights at the west entrance to Munising Harbor were in danger of being forever forgotten until just a few years ago. But thanks to the conscientious endeavors of the U.S. Forest Service, these lights have been rescued.

The front range light is a small steel cylinder situated close to the shore of Lake Superior. Its white surface has been

END OF THE ROAD REAR RANGE LIGHT

marred by graffiti, but the structure is still sound.

Inland, on the other side of the highway, the white top of the rear range light stands out from the deep greens of the surrounding forest. As you move closer, the black bottom of the conical steel structure also comes into view. A door nearly halfway up the side indicates that at one time a dwelling may have been attached to the tower, with entry at its second story.

When we visited, small windows on either side of the tower were open, and we looked in at a very interesting sight. Unlike at nearly all other lighthouses, whose staircases are supported by a central pole, the staircase here is the exact opposite. Supports for the steps are attached to the outer wall, and the staircase ascends without its sides touching either the wall or a central support. Brackets from the wall extend out to help support the staircase, and a few cross beams support landings.

Recently, the U.S. Coast Guard granted a request from the Munising Boat Club to relight the structure. The Coast Guard installed a new light, and the Upper Peninsula Power Company re-ran electricity to the tower free of charge. The light is shining once again, thanks to the Munising Boat Club and many other local volunteers.

And since it is located in the village of Christmas, the light is appropriately decorated each year during that special season, a new tradition to honor the antique beacon.

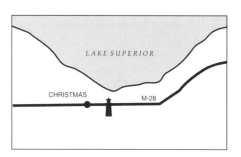

DIRECTIONS: From M-28 in Christmas, about halfway between Bay Furnace Campground and the Munising Tourist Park, turn south onto a trail road and you will see the End of the Road Rear Range light in front of you. The End of the Road Front Range Light is directly across M-28, at the water's edge.

69/70 MUNISING RANGE LIGHTS

The Munising Range Lights are still in use today. The front range light is in a white, steel-plated conical tower about 50 feet high, with a white parapet surrounding an octagonal lantern. A red ventilator ball and a United States flag flying from the parapet provide the only color.

The rear range is farther inland, uphill from the front range, and it too is white, steel-plated and conical. But since it is at a more elevated location, it is a much shorter tower, standing only about 30 feet high. A single lantern panel gives the light access to the lake far below.

FRONT RANGE LIGHT

REAR RANGE LIGHT

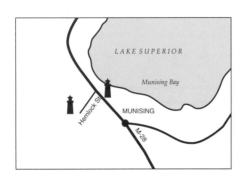

DIRECTIONS: The Munising Front Range Light is on M-28 in Munising, about 2 blocks east of the high school on the north side of the street. Directly across M-28 from the front range light is Hemlock St. To see the Munising Rear Range Light, follow Hemlock about two blocks to its end.

GRAND ISLAND NORTH LIGHTHOUSE 71

In 1990 Grand Island was designated a National Recreation Area, which finally opened up the unique offshore parcel to the public. Making access even easier is a passenger ferry that now makes twice-daily trips out of Munising during the summer months.

As Tom Powers says in his guide, *Natural Michigan*, "Most visitors come away from a trip to ... (this) ... island agreeing that nature has created one of the most beautiful spots in the world." Even the original inhabitants, the Ojibway Indians, passed over the mainland in favor of settling on the island, only a mile and a half north across Munising Bay from Powell Point. At various times since, it's been used for timber and maple syrup production and as a corporate retreat for the Cleveland Cliffs Iron Company, which bought the entire island in 1901.

In 1990 the federal government purchased the eight-mile-long, three-mile-wide island and opened it to public use. The diverse nature of the area — including sandy beaches, caves, waterfalls, towering hardwood forests and two lighthouses — invite you to spend as much time as possible, but facilities at this time are minimal. Hiking is a wonderful way to explore the island's nooks and crannies, and primitive camping is allowed. On our first trip, we toured with mountain bikes which, unlike other types, don't get bogged down in sandy areas and more easily climb up the rugged hills.

All of the buildings on the island, except the ranger station, are privately owned, including the Grand Island North Point Lighthouse. This light is used as a private home, and respect must be shown to the residents. Sitting high atop a sand-stone bluff that borders large sections of the island, the beautiful, yellow house has been well-preserved. Dormer windows peek out from the second story, and green shutters trim the windows on both the house and tower. The square tower is connected to the house, but also has its own door leading directly outside. The tower is topped with a block lantern room and roof, and the black iron walkway surrounding the top must make an ideal place for a peaceful evening of relaxation.

Because of the lighthouse's position on the bluff, it can only be seen from the water quite a distance offshore. Because of the unpredictable nature of Superior that far out, we don't recommend that you visit this light in a small boat. On land there is one spot on the northern end of the island where you can get a view of the lighthouse, although you are a great distance from it. Since the future development of Grand Island will, no doubt, include more trails, this light may become more approachable. So ask the rangers at the station near the island ferry dock for the best way to view this light.

The *Island Hopper* offers ferry service to Grand Island, with four departure times daily through the summer months and reduced service through mid-October. For a current schedule, call the cruise service at (906) 387-3503 during the summer months or the Visitors Center and Park Headquarters in Munising, (906) 387-3700, year round.

For more information on Grand Island, write Hiawatha National Forest, Munising Ranger District, 400 E. Munising Ave., Munising, MI 49862.

72 GRAND ISLAND EAST CHANNEL LIGHTHOUSE

The Grand Island East Channel Lighthouse is on the southeast shore of Grand Island. You can see it from the decks of either a Pictured Rocks Cruise boat, as it heads from Munising Harbor to the national lakeshore area, or from a private boat. Though Grand Island is a designated National Recreation Area and is now much more accessible to the public, the lighthouse itself remains on private property.

Long abandoned, the lighthouse was in danger of crumbling to the ground until just a few years ago, when a group of private citizens, including the owner, decided to do something about it. They repaired its stone foundation and supported the tower and house with a series of cables. Now a much sturdier building rests on the sandy shoreline of the island, the sapphire waters of Munising Bay lapping at its feet and the shaded greens of the forest framing its back.

Its deep-brown foundation shows signs of the repairs, but its wood siding has not seen a trace of paint or other decoration. The wood has weathered to a dark gray, and the square tower is capped with a dome of green copper roofing, long exposed to the elements.

The best views of this light come while aboard a glass-bottomed tour boat that glides over some of the area's most spectacular sunken ships. For more information on these fascinating excursions, which depart out of Munising, call Shipwreck Tours, Inc. at (906) 387-4477. You can also see the light from the popular Pictured Rocks boat cruises, which offer daily trips throughout the summer. Call (906) 387-2379 for more information.

AU SABLE POINT LIGHTHOUSE 73

The Pictured Rocks National Lakeshore is one of the crown jewels of Michigan's Upper Peninsula. In the center of the park, at Au Sable Point, a secluded lighthouse compound snuggles close to the Lake Superior shore. Vehicles are not allowed out to the point, so you must make an easy 1½-mile walk to the lighthouse from the beautiful Hurricane River area. From the dark waters of the Hurricane River eastward, the big lake's shore is lined with large boulders and the layered sandstone shelf that borders so much of the Pictured Rocks.

When we first visited the lighthouse, in the summer of 1986, the lake levels were unusually low. Instead of following the well-worn trail on the bluff above the lake, we were able to walk down on the lakeshore itself. We crossed over boulders and through sections of water, quickly becoming soaked but refreshed by the beauty and serenity of the area. We occasionally heard voices passing by on the route atop the bluff seven feet above us, but we had the entire shore to ourselves.

Today, the lake levels are much higher, and we recommend staying on the trail, a two-track road, that leads to the lighthouse. Thick forest lines both sides of the road, but you can catch glimpses of the lake, to the north, through the green leaves, which provide much-appreciated shade on hot, sunny days and a break from the wind on cool days.

This active, though secluded, light station was put into service in 1874. In 1958 the beacon was automated and the property turned over to the National Park Service, which is in the process of restoring the lighthouse. The white tower, the large, attached red-brick keeper's dwelling, and a matching red-brick fog signal building are still standing. The tower stretches skyward, a streak of white against the deep blue of the sunny sky, and its empty lantern is bordered by a black parapet and cap.

The light's Third Order Fresnel lens, once housed in the nearby Nautical and Maritime Museum in Grand Marais, has been brought home to the tower. Though the park service has closed and boarded up all the outbuildings to protect them as they prepare for renovation, the lighthouse itself has been restored and is open for summer tours. Call (906) 494-2669 for a schedule.

Some standing trees border the lighthouse with green, while below the tower the plunging sides of the sandy embankment are covered with trees and bushes toppled over in a heap. Visible beyond the lighthouse to the east, the magnificent Grand Sable Banks make a sweeping march to Superior, where their soft browns tumble below the blue waters.

Several shipwrecks have washed ashore near the lighthouse. The raging of the lake has left only their scarred hulls, with waves now crashing over exposed ends of huge timbers half buried in the wet sand. Although these wrecks are more than a century old, they are a sobering reminder of the power of the lake and its effect on those unfortunate enough to be caught in its sweeping fury.

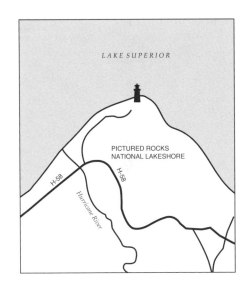

DIRECTIONS: Drive to the Hurricane River Campground, in the Pictured Rocks National Lakeshore just north off H-58 about 39 miles northeast of Munising or about 13 miles west of Grand Marais. As you enter the campground, park near the Hurricane River and walk to the far end of the campground to a two-track road near the lake with a gate across it. Follow this trail close to the lakeshore about 1.5 miles east to the lighthouse.

AU SABLE POINT LIGHTHOUSE

GRAND MARAIS HARBOR RANGE LIGHTS 74

weeping west to east from shore out into Lake Superior at Grand Marais is a large piece of sandy land that helps both form and protect the beautiful harbor there. A stone pier that probes Lake Superior from the end of that peninsula marks the location of the Grand Marais Harbor Range Lights. The front range light rests on the end of the pier, and the rear range light is on shore.

Their designs are similar. Both sit on a steel skeleton with a square steel-sided room at the top. The Rear Range Light also has a parapet and octagonal lantern room above the steel enclosure.

Just across the street from the Rear Range is the Grand Marais lifesaving station, which has been preserved and now houses the Pictured Rocks National Lakeshore Nautical and Maritime Museum. A lookout tower still surveys the sandy shoreline surrounding the harbor. The Third Order Fresnel lens from the Au Sable Point light is on display inside the museum, but it is slated to be returned to its home when that lighthouse's renovation is completed, in the next few years. The museum is open July 1 through Labor Day, 10 a.m. to 6 p.m. The schedule is subject to change, so call (906) 494-2669 to check on current hours.

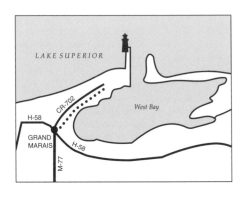

DIRECTIONS: From the junction of M-77, H-58, and County Rd. 702 in downtown Grand Marais, turn northeast onto CR-702 and follow it about ½ mile to its end at a large parking area near the museum and range lights.

75 CRISP POINT LIGHT

Crisp Point is on a remote section of land that juts out slightly into Lake Superior between the tiny near-ghost towns of Two Heart and Vermillion. Because of its isolation and difficult access, this lighthouse is rarely visited, and you will probably have the beautiful area entirely to yourself.

From the beach in front of the light, it's hard not to feel the loneliness that must have plagued the men stationed here. The sandy shoreline is unbroken — no houses, harbors or docks — in both directions as far as the eye can see. A dark line of forest follows the strip of sand, beach grasses and low bushes provide other greenery, and the beach is littered with gnarled driftwood.

The lighthouse stands only a few yards from the icy blue water in an area where the trees thin out and dunes take over. In front of the lighthouse, the remains of old docks that used to service the light station stretch out into the waters off the point. Today, just their foundations appear above the water line, the huge wooden poles touching the waves that pass by.

At the lighthouse itself, white paint has peeled from the brick tower in several large areas, but the attached one-story building has taken the brunt of nature's fury. Its foundation, undermined by waves, collapsed in November 1996. That same year the Crisp Point Light was put on the Most Endangered list published by *Lighthouse Digest* out of Wells, Maine.

The Crisp Point Lighthouse Historical Society, with the help of three major donors—Bay Mills Indian Community, Sault Ste. Marie Tribe of Chippewa Indians, and Spencer Mursey Jr.—was able to offer what remains of this light station a little more security in the form of boulders strewn in front of the tower to decrease the constant danger of erosion. Interested individuals may contact this organization by writing to The Crisp Point Lighthouse Historical Society, P.O. Box 229, Paradise, MI 49768 or phoning (906) 492-3206.

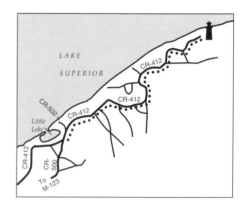

DIRECTIONS: Although surrounded by private land, the owner has generously allowed access to Crisp Point, with restrictions being no fires, RVs or camping.

Approximately 5 miles west of the entrance to Upper Tahquamenon Falls on M-123 (about 18.5 miles north of Newberry), turn north onto County Rd. 500 and go about 12.2 miles to County Rd. 412. Turn right (east) onto CR-412 and follow it about 7 miles to the lighthouse parking area. At about 4.5 miles, CR-412 turns north and becomes a narrow trail. We recommend that during periods of wet weather you attempt the trip in nothing less than a two-wheel drive truck.

Though CR-412 is clearly marked all the way to the parking area, the route around Little Lake can be confusing. After you turn east from CR-500 onto CR-412, the road that follows the east shore of Little Lake is CR-502 and you might see a sign for that road before the sign for CR-412. Just follow CR-502 as you curve around the lake, and look for the sign for CR-412, which branches off to the east.

When you reach the parking area, walk down to the beach and you will see the lighthouse about ¼ mile away, to the east. You can either walk down the beach itself or on an old, sandy trail just inside the tree line.

WHITEFISH POINT LIGHT 76

First lit in 1849, the Whitefish Point Light shares honors with that at Copper Harbor for being the first lights on Lake Superior.

Whitefish Point was an important navigational point on Lake Superior. It marked the entrance to Whitefish Bay, sometimes the only shelter to be found for a ship trying to escape the fury of the lake. Today, the bay still serves that critical role, and the light, now automated, still shines forth from the tower, ready to assist if needed.

Though the tower that stands today replaced the original tower during the Civil War, the 80-foot-tall structure has a very functional, modern appearance. An iron skeleton with a very wide base gradually narrows to support a central steel cylinder. The narrow cylinder in turn supports the octagonal parapet and lantern room above. A red dome caps the lantern. The surrounding buildings were once home to the Coast Guard personnel stationed at this light and responsible for its maintenance.

In a large, stark-white wood-sided building nearby, the Great Lakes Shipwreck Historical Society has opened the Great Lakes Shipwreck Museum. A collection of artifacts combines with brief descriptions to tell the touching stories of several of the hundreds of shipwrecks that have taken place in the "Graveyard of the Great Lakes," off the shores of Whitefish Point. Regular showings of colorful underwater films explain the shipwrecks from a diver's-eye view, and a Second Order Fresnel lens from White Shoals is on display. The museum is open from Memorial Day through October 15, seven days a week, 10 a.m. to 6 p.m. There is a small admission fee.

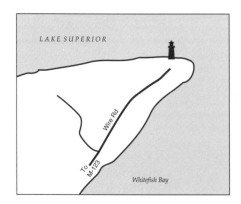

LAKE SUPERIOR

Wire Rd

To M-123

Whitefish Bay

DIRECTIONS: From where M-123 makes a 90-degree turn at the north end of Paradise, turn north onto Wire Rd. and follow it about 11 miles.

77 POINT IROQUOIS LIGHTHOUSE

The Point Iroquois light was first illuminated in 1857 and its Fourth Order Fresnel lens shone over one of the busiest shipping lanes in the world — the entrance to the St. Mary's River and the Soo Locks.

Point Iroquois became busier with each passing year, and the personnel and facilities required to run the station grew accordingly. In 1870 the house and tower were completely rebuilt, and after the turn of the century, the living space was enlarged to house the head keeper, two assistant keepers, and their families. That also created quite a group of children at the station, and in time the government was persuaded to sponsor a school at the point. The children of a local fisherman also attended, and the point became a meeting place of sorts for nearby residents.

One of the children who spent nearly all of her childhood at the Point Iroquois Lighthouse was Betty Byrnes Bacon, and she later wrote a wonderful narrative of her life at the point, *Lighthouse Memories: Growing Up at Point Iroquois in the 1920s.* Betty's story is so full of life, you are constantly reminded that not only was this an official facility, with all of its rules and regulations, but it was also sim-

ilar to an old fashioned homestead, where residents had to preserve food, chop wood, and pump up cold water to be heated for baths in front of a roaring fire. Dog sleds, sleigh rides, and rum runners trying to slip across the river from Canada were all a part of life here, and the beautiful natural surroundings provided what almost all children raised in lighthouses have said is the best playground a child could have.

For more than 100 years, the Point Iroquois Light performed its duties flawlessly, but in 1962, its light was extinguished in favor of a beacon farther out in the water.

Today, the lighthouse and tower have been renovated thanks to the concerted and cooperative efforts of the Bay Mills/Brimley Historical Research Society and the current land owner, the National Forest Service. The lighthouse, now a part of the Hiawatha National Forest, rests on a small, sandy bluff above Lake Superior, and the shore here is littered with unusual driftwood and multicolored stones. Wildflowers fill the clearings, and the lighthouse is partially obstructed by tall bushes and pines that have grown unchallenged. The large two-story house is white, with a red roof sloping over all the gables and additions. The attached brick tower, also white, is topped with a black parapet and lantern room.

The historical society has renovated the interior of the house, and antiques and memorabilia have been arranged to show what life was like during this lighthouse's heyday. Informative displays fill several rooms, and the gift shop sells lighthouse-theme souvenirs and a wide variety of books on Michigan's nautical and natural

history, including *Lighthouse Memories.* The museum and gift shop are open from Memorial Day through October 15. Hours are Monday through Thursday, 10 a.m. to 5 p.m. and Friday, Saturday and Sunday, 10 a.m. to 5 p.m. and 7 p.m. to 9 p.m. Hours may vary so call (906) 437-5272 for a current schedule.

The 65-foot tower is also open to the public during those times. From its top you have a commanding view of the sandy shoreline as it stretches out of sight, and of Canada, across the water to the north.

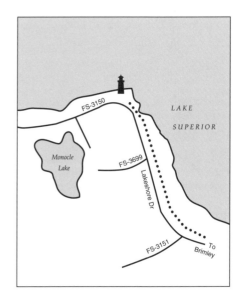

DIRECTIONS: In Brimley where M-221 dead-ends at Lake Superior, turn left onto 6 Mile Rd. (called Lakeshore Dr. near the lighthouse) and go about 7.5 miles.

POINT IROQUOIS LIGHTHOUSE

ROUND ISLAND REAR RANGE LIGHT 78

This light, which is on private property, has recently collapsed and cannot be seen from the water.

79 MIDDLE NEEBISH FRONT RANGE LIGHT

On the north end of Neebish Island, facing the St. Mary's River channel utilized by downbound ships headed for Lake Huron, stands the Middle Neebish Range Light, one of the very few original range lights remaining from the 1800s.

The narrow, 40-foot-tall metal tower supports a large, red metal sign with a white vertical stripe running down its center. That day marker is still used by ships, and the light atop the tower is also still working.

All around, remnants of past use lay in discarded heaps, from a steel contraption that looks to have been a chair of some type to abandoned strips of track that were used to run supplies up from a small cement pier, which has toppled over into the shallow waters at the base of the light.

Several hundred yards out from shore is another active range light, called "The Chair" because of its distinctive shape.

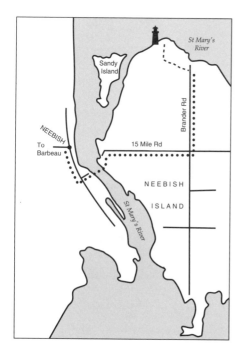

DIRECTIONS: From Barbeau, about 15 miles south of Sault Ste. Marie, take the main road east 2.7 miles to Neebish. Turn right (south) and go 0.4 miles to the Neebish Island Ferry Dock, at the end of a short road to the left.

After crossing the river, from the dock area on Neebish Island, follow Ferry Rd. 0.3 miles to 15 mile Rd. Turn right (east) onto 15 Mile and go about 2.2 miles to Brander Rd. Turn left (north) onto Brander and go approximately 1.9 miles to a trail, marked by power lines, on the left. Park near the main road and follow the trail and power lines on foot west about one mile to where the power lines turn north. Follow them north, less than ½ mile, to the front range light, on the river's shore.

78

ROUND ISLAND LIGHTHOUSE 80

On the east shore of Round Island, which dots the turquoise waters of the St. Mary's River between Point Aux Frenes and Lime Island, a lighthouse stands watch over the shipping lanes. Though built before the turn of the century, the Round Island Lighthouse is still a very sturdy structure. A dark stone base has provided a secure foundation for the two-story wood dwelling and attached wood tower. The square three-story tower dominates the front side of the house, and the first-story windows of both have been boarded up. A lone window stares out from the third story of the tower, and above that, the parapet is lined with a black iron railing. A black cap and ventilator ball tops the six-sided lantern room, which is now empty. Nearby, a skeletal steel tower is topped by a still-active automated light.

A weathered outbuilding hides behind the lighthouse, and the woods surrounding the structures are beginning to reclaim the once-cleared land. A cement breakwater in front of the lighthouse still protects it from erosion. The shore of the island is lined with small pebbles and long pieces of driftwood, which have found a resting place just inches away from the swift-flowing river.

81 DeTour Reef Light

DeTour Reef Light, built on a reef in the south entrance waters of the St. Mary's River, is well-preserved and bears few marks of abuse by the elements. The sturdy concrete platform that supports the structure rises about 20 feet from the surface of the water. A small wire railing frames its edge, and thick iron rings attached close to the water level allow Coast Guard ships to dock.

The light's white steel tower rises in three distinct levels from that concrete platform. The first level is a large, square two-story base interrupted by several windows, some of which are blocked up or painted over. The base is trimmed at its top, in places, with a black cast-iron fence. The second level, still square but much narrower, rises another two stories and has only a few narrow windows. The third level — which not only narrows again, but also becomes ten-sided — rises only about another 10 feet to support the light. A walkway, enclosed by a black iron fence, surrounds both of the upper levels. The light itself is enclosed by a window consisting of several small, square panes and is capped by an orange steel dome.

The DeTour Reef Light Preservation Society has been working since January 1998 to save this light for generations to come. Anyone interested in contacting that group can write them at P.O. Box 519, DeTour Village, MI 49725 or call (906) 297-8888.

MARTIN REEF LIGHT 82

About seven miles southeast of the Les Cheneaux Islands, the rocky Lake Huron bottom rises close enough to the surface that you can see it from a boat. Since 1927 a light has stood on the dangerous area, called Martin Reef, to warn boat travelers on the busy water highway connecting the Straits and the St. Mary's River.

The concrete platform rises about 17 feet from water level and is edged on top by gentle arcs of the drooping sections of a white chain fence. Rising from its center is a large, square three-story building, whose white steel-plate siding is broken on each side by four rectangular windows, each divided into many smaller panes. Jutting up from the base structure is a small, square 10-foot-high tower crowned by a white iron railing that surrounds the light, which is capped by an orange dome.

83 SPECTACLE REEF LIGHT

The year 1867 was particularly unlucky for ships trying to navigate the Spectacle Reef area, in Lake Huron about 11 miles east of the Straits. With no light to warn them of the reef, which is only seven feet from the surface at its shallowest, two ships ran into the rocky shoals that year. As a result, it wasn't hard to convince Congress to erect a permanent light at this location, even though the cost was estimated to be a formidable $300,000-$400,000 (about 3-4 million 1995 dollars).

In 1870 work began on what would be one of the most difficult lighthouses to build on the Great Lakes. Before they could even begin construction, workers first had to remove the wreckage and cargo of one of the recently downed ships from the reef. The base of operations was at Les Cheneaux, 16 miles northwest, which made transportation of materials and work crews a problem. The light was designed as a crib structure, with the crib being made on land in four sections and then shipped over when completed. Ice played a major part in hampering efforts. One spring, workers had to chop through 30 feet of massive ice sheets before they could get inside the tower. And every spring they found that the incredible buildup of ice over the winter months had eroded the light's foundation. After several improvements the underwater walls were expanded to a thickness of 20 feet, tapering off to six feet near the top.

It took four years to complete the structure, and today the original limestone tower stands as a monument to perseverance and dedication. Its light, now solar-powered, still warns ships of the spectacle-shaped reef lurking below. The conical tower is 95 feet high, with a single row of small windows lining up from bottom to top, and its light-tan color makes it unique among the other area lights. It is capped by an orange dome, and a small, white building attached to the base of the tower also has an orange roof. Paint is chipping off the sides of the building, leaving a hodgepodge of white, green and orange along its sides. The top half of the concrete platform is steel-sided, and the absence of people makes it a perfect perch for the numerous gulls in the area.

BOIS BLANC ISLAND LIGHTHOUSE 84

The first lighthouse on Bois Blanc Island was built in 1829, but bad planning made it necessary to rebuild much earlier than expected. In 1837 when a wild storm blew in off the lake, Emily Ward, the lightkeeper's daughter, was at the lighthouse with only a young relative. Because the light was built too close to the shore, it was in imminent danger of being undermined by the waves. Sensing this, Emily ran up and down the tower's 150 stairs, bringing down not only the lamp but also the fragile reflectors. Just after she had finished her fifth and final trip, the tower broke apart and fell into the churning water below.

In 1867 another lighthouse was built in the same general location — on a long, narrow peninsula that juts out from the island's north side — but much farther back from shore. Today, an even-newer tower, just north of the old one, houses an automated light, and the old structure is now a private residence.

The two-story light-brick dwelling is pretty, but it is the attached tower that catches your eye and keeps it. Jutting out from the front of the house, the square brick tower dominates the architecture of the building. Overlooking the water, the face of the tower has a door at its base and two large windows on its second and third levels. Large, square panes surround the 10-sided lantern room, which is capped with a white roof and ventilator ball.

Orange shutters, which border all of the tower and house windows, are functional as well as decorative and can be closed when the house is not in use or to shut out cold, icy blasts from the lake. A narrow sidewalk that leads from the cen-ter of the tower down to the shore has been washed away and otherwise damaged in some areas.

Pines tower above the simple struc-ture, and in a brush of deep greens, the forest sweeps past the lighthouse down to the rocky shore.

85 ROUND ISLAND LIGHTHOUSE

Round Island Lighthouse is probably the most-viewed lighthouse in Michigan. Perched at the end of a sandy point, it faces nearby Mackinac Island, and dozens of ferries loaded with day-trippers bound for that popular tourist destination glide past each summer day.

But Round Island is the opposite of busy Mackinac. It is a complete wilderness, part of the Hiawatha National Forest, reachable only by boat or across solid ice. Early Mackinac Island residents crossed to Round Island and cut so much wood that they depleted the growth that created the remarkably arched skyline responsible for the island's name.

Although dates from several sources conflict, it is safe to say that the current lighthouse was built in 1895-96. By the late 1940s, a channel light closer to Mackinac Island made this lighthouse obsolete, and it was abandoned. Over the following years, the structure fell into terrible disrepair and was close to collapse. Finally, in the late 1970s, a cooperative effort of local citizens and government agencies resulted in the restoration and protection of the lighthouse.

As a result, today the lighthouse is one of the most picturesque in the area. The three-story brick structure stands at the end of a narrow finger of sand, which pokes from the island's northwest shore, and is surrounded by the turquoise waters of the Straits. The bottom level of the house is painted brick-red and its upper stories pristine white. The entire tower, which raises out of the northwest corner of the house, is painted red and is capped by a black cast-iron parapet. All window trim and doors plus the platform on which the building stands have also been painted black.

In 1995, restoration efforts were continued by Boy Scout Troop 323 from Freeland, Michigan, in conjunction with the Great Lakes Lighthouse Keepers Association. The Scouts' reputation for perseverance has withstood even the 90 mph winds that greeted their first night on the island. The troop went on to remove more than three tons of plaster and debris in their first year of work, and plans include complete restoration of the structure.

CHEBOYGAN RIVER FRONT RANGE LIGHTHOUSE

86

The Cheboygan River Front Range light, built in 1880, rises up from the roof line of a white two-story house near the marina on the Cheboygan River. The square tower sits atop the wood dwelling, which used to house the men stationed at the light but is no longer in service. Government workers still use the building, however, and it is not open to the public.

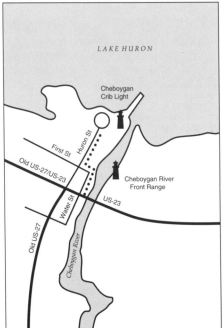

DIRECTIONS: To visit the Cheboygan River Front Range Lighthouse, from the junction of US-23 and Old US-27, at a traffic signal in downtown Cheboygan, go one block east on US-23 to Water St., the last street before the drawbridge. Turn left (north) onto Water St., go about one block, and look for the large range light building on your right, adjacent to a Bois Blanc Island boat dock.

To get to the Cheboygan Crib Light, continue north on Water St. about one more block to where it turns left (west) onto First St. Go two blocks on First to Huron St. Turn right (north) onto Huron and go about ½ mile to Gordon Turner Park.

87 CHEBOYGAN CRIB LIGHT

Why is the Cheboygan Crib Light standing on land when the very nature of a "crib" implies that it be offshore? A wood box — a "crib" — is constructed as a base, then filled with large rocks that are later covered with concrete to form a solid foundation for a light.

At one time the Cheboygan Crib Light was, in fact, set offshore to help guide boats into the Cheboygan River. But its foundation continuously settled until, finally, the entire structure tipped over into the channel.

But instead of destroying the no-longer-useful beacon, the people of Cheboygan pulled it ashore and gave it a new home at the beginning of a short pier on the west bank of the rivermouth. The circular steel tower, only about 25 feet tall, is charming because of its small dimensions. The building, which is not open to the public, has been freshly painted white, with a red parapet and red trim on the windows and their protruding sills.

The city has also beautified the sur-rounding area, and a new boardwalk leads from the pier west along the shore of Lake Huron to a public beach and park, which has plenty of picnic tables. The beautiful, sandy beach attracts swimmers, and a nature trail is just a short distance away. The pier itself, which extends out only about 300 feet into Lake Huron, is a magnet for boat watchers, who view the continuous parade of vessels in and out the river entrance.

(Map and DIRECTIONS, page 85.)

OLD CHEBOYGAN LIGHTHOUSE RUINS 88

The ruins of the Old Cheboygan Lighthouse are located in Cheboygan State Park, and the 1¼-mile walk to them is beautiful. The low-lying path is surrounded by towering cedar and scattered hardwoods, and when the wide trail occasionally rises, the cedars give way to thick oak, maple, popple and spruce. As you near the ruins, you can walk to them either along the beach or through a cedar swamp. Both trails are well-marked and easy to follow.

After the lighthouse was abandoned in the 1920s, vandals damaged the buildings to the extent that they became unsafe and had to be torn down. Low stone walls still stand in some places, and it is possible to discern the perimeter of what once was the entire building. Red bricks are scattered throughout the bushes and tall grasses, and a sidewalk still leads down to the beach.

Along the beach, you can get good views of two other lighthouses that still guide ships through the area waters. To the northeast, some three miles off the eastern tip of Bois Blanc Island, is the Poe Reef Light. To the northwest is Fourteen Foot Shoal Light. This is the closest you can get to these lights without a boat.

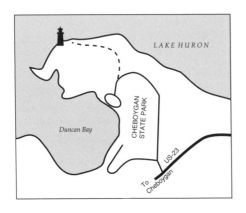

DIRECTIONS: From the junction of US-23 and Old US-27, at a traffic signal in downtown Cheboygan, go east on US-23 approximately 3.8 miles to Cheboygan State Park, on the left (north). Enter the park (daily or annual permit required) and take the right (north) fork of the park road about 1.6 miles to the campgrounds. The walking trail to the lighthouse ruins starts about 150 yards before the campground office. You can pick up a trail map at either the campground office or the trailhead. The route is well-marked and fairly easy to follow.

About halfway along the 1.3-mile walk, the trail intersects a narrow sand road. Follow that road to the left (west) about ¼ mile to another road — marked by a wood post gate beyond this junction — that heads to the right (north). Follow the right-hand fork about one block to where you first see 14 Foot Shoal Cabin. In this area look for a trail to the left (west) and follow it less than ¼ mile to a clearing, where you will pass by an ancient apple tree and then reach a sidewalk that takes you a few yards to what is left of the lighthouse.

You can also reach the ruins by continuing down the road past 14 Foot Shoal Cabin to the beach and then walking left (west) down the beach less than ¼ mile to the ruins, marked by a large wood sign up on the sand bank to the left.

89 FOURTEEN FOOT SHOAL LIGHT

Fourteen Foot Shoal Light, about 1½ miles off the shore of Lake Huron near Cheboygan, is not large. Its concrete base rises from the blue water only about 10 feet, but it provides a strong foundation for the small, white, square building at its center. From the hip roof of that one-story steel-plated building, the cylindrical steel tower rises about 15 additional feet and is capped in red cast iron.

This light was never manned. Rather, the crew stationed at Poe Reef Light, about 3½ miles away, used a radio beacon to control the lamp and fog signal. The Fourteen Foot shoal structure could, however, provide shelter for maintenance crews trapped there by foul weather.

You can get a good view of this light from the Cheboygan Light ruins, at Cheboygan State Park.

POE REEF LIGHT 90

Prior to the construction of the Poe Reef Light, in 1929, this dangerous area, about two miles offshore north of Cheboygan, was marked only by lightships.

This light is in very good shape, and its distinctive black and white bands make it seem larger than it really is. The building rests on a concrete platform edged by a fence that kept residents here within safe boundaries. Rising from this base is a square three-story building, topped by a slightly narrower, square fourth story and then the light, which is capped by a red-domed roof. The bottom level is painted black, a thick band of white outlines the second and third stories, and the narrower top level is also black.

The wonder of this and other lights that rest in the water is found not only above the surface, but also below the level of the cool blueness lapping at the sides of your boat. When visiting Poe Reef, you can see the large rocks, resting on the bottom, that create such a hazard to ships trying to navigate through the area. You can get a distant view of the Poe Reef light from Gordon Turner Park, in Cheboygan, and a much closer look from the shore of Lake Huron at Cheboygan State Park.

91 FORTY MILE POINT LIGHTHOUSE

A small county park that hugs the shoreline north of Rogers City shelters another of Michigan's no-longer-used lighthouses. But Forty Mile Point Lighthouse, originally built in 1897 and rebuilt in 1935, is far from abandoned. Far-sighted individuals have beautifully preserved the lighthouse, which is on display in Presque Isle County's Lighthouse Park, near P.H. Hoeft State Park.

The square, white three-story tower rises from a reddish-brown brick wall of the two-story keeper's house. The tower is topped by an octagonal lantern room, with a delicate black fence surrounding its square walkway. Very narrow windows rise in pairs up the face of the first two levels, and the third story features one thin window on the front and sides.

Adjacent to the tower on each side, dormer windows peep out from the large house's black-shingled roof with contrasting white eaves and bracing beneath. White trim also accents the windows, which are topped with gray stone headers. The grounds are well-maintained, and several beautiful shade trees dot the lawn. The well-preserved fog whistle building is nearby.

A visit to the lighthouse is a popular stopover for families. From nature trails winding through shady woodlands to a half-buried shipwreck just west of the lighthouse, an afternoon's visit passes quickly among these fascinating remnants of history.

The 40 Mile Point Lighthouse Society, caretakers of this light, can be reached at P.O. Box 205, Rogers City, MI 49779.

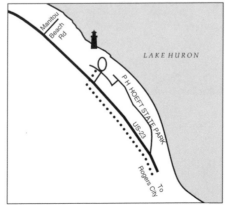

DIRECTIONS: From the junction of US-23 and M-68, near Rogers City, go north on US-23 approximately 6.2 miles to an unmarked "Presque Isle County Lighthouse Park." (The unmarked road, with a steel gate by the highway, is 2 miles north of P.H. Hoeft State Park and is not 40 Mile Point Rd., which you will also pass.) Follow the short road about one block to a "T" intersection. A parking area is to the right and the lighthouse is to the left.

OLD AND NEW PRESQUE ISLE LIGHTHOUSES

92/93

PRESQUE ISLE OLD RANGE LIGHTS

94/95

Presque Isle is a thin strip of land along Lake Huron between Alpena and Rogers City that is nearly split from the mainland by Grand Lake. Only at the northwest and southeast shores of the long, narrow inland lake is Presque Isle connected to the mainland, which is the reason for its name, "nearly an island."

Poking out into Lake Huron from the north shore of Presque Isle is a small finger of land that helps form Presque Isle Harbor. That beautiful peninsula, covered with cedars and pines, is home to the area's two major lighthouses.

Old Presque Isle Light was built near the base of the peninsula in 1840 and gave 30 hard years of service before being replaced and abandoned. But this lighthouse was later rescued from the ravages of time by far-sighted individuals, and it is now a museum open to the public.

The white brick keeper's cottage is utterly quaint and charming, from its peaked cedar-shake roof to the front porch, raised a few feet by walls of large field stones. Open to the sunshine and cooling breezes blowing in from Lake Huron, the stoop must have been a favorite spot to relax as afternoons dipped toward evenings.

Inside is the museum, and it's filled with period pieces from the 1800s — including one upstairs room completely renovated by a local Girl Scout troop — that give excellent glimpses into the house's past. It is well worth the small admission fee to view the house plus the collection of nautical antiques and shipwreck information.

The two-story conical tower is also open. Its white brick walls are four feet thick at the bottom, and its sturdy look carries through to the black parapet and lantern room at the top. Its most unusual feature is the hand-chiseled stone staircase, which you can climb, that winds upward to the light.

There are several items in the museum and on the surrounding property that you can experiment with, including a captain's sextant and a huge bronze bell from the old Lansing City Hall. Tall cedars stretch upward from the base of the tower to shade it with their deep greens, and the corners of the keeper's dwelling are also accented with the beautiful trees. The wide expanses of lawn and beautiful, nearby beaches make this a wonderful place to stop for a peaceful picnic.

One mile north of the old light is the beacon that replaced it, the New Presque Isle Light, built in 1870. The road to it is bordered on both sides by heavy growth of tall cedars and pines, and as you near

OLD FRONT RANGE LIGHT

91

the end of the drive, the huge, white tower commands your view.

And for good reason. At more than 100 feet tall measured from the ground and higher measured from the water, this is one of the tallest light structures on the Great Lakes. The conical brick tower has a few black-trimmed windows scattered along its stairway, and a row of small, arched windows peek out from just beneath the walkway. The decorative trim of the walkway is black, and the lantern is capped in red.

This light, which houses its original Third Order Fresnel lens, is still in service, but the tower is opened to the public twice a year, on the Saturdays of the 4th of July and Labor Day weekends. Call (517) 734-4138 for further information.

The attached keeper's dwelling is much larger than that at the older light-house. The two-story brick structure, with dormer windows looming out from the peaked roof, must have been quite a step up for the family that moved from the older lighthouse to this "modern" dwelling in the early 1870s. This building, too, now houses a museum, with two floors of period furnishings plus a gift shop you won't want to miss.

The Old Presque Isle and New Presque Isle museums have the same schedule, from mid-May through mid-October, seven days a week, 9 a.m. to 6 p.m.

The New Presque Isle Light is the centerpiece of what is now called Lighthouse Park, which also includes a large picnic area with a pavilion. A wide expanse of well-kept lawn, dotted with a few large trees, stretches from the lighthouse complex to the edge of the surrounding forest. The waters of Lake Huron are never far away, and be sure to enjoy the numerous nature trails in the area. Every July 4th the park is the site of a large picnic and barbeque that is open to the public.

Near the entrance road to the Old Presque Isle Lighthouse is the Old Front Range Light, which was moved many years ago from its original home near the Old Rear Range Light.

The old Rear Range Light, near Harbor View, is also no longer in service and is a private residence. The white wood siding is interrupted on all sides by small, lovely arched windows, and it's unusual smaller-than-normal second story is still topped by the range light.

DIRECTIONS: From US-23 approximately 13.7 miles southeast of Rogers City, turn east onto 638 Hwy./Highway Rd. and go about 2 miles to where 638 Hwy. and Hwy. Rd. split. Go left (east) on 638 Hwy. about 1.9 miles to Grand Lake Rd. (County Rd. 405). Turn left (north) onto Grand Lake Rd. (CR-405) and go about 0.7 miles to the Lake Huron shore. In that area, look for a beach on the right and the beach parking area on the left. The Old Presque Isle Rear Range Light is behind this parking lot, and although it is a private residence, you can get a glimpse of it from CR-405.

Continue north on Grand Lake Rd. (CR-405) another 0.2 miles and look for the old Presque Isle Front Range Light, on the right. Turn right (east) into the driveway next to this light and follow it to the Old Presque Isle Lighthouse Museum. The new Presque Isle Lighthouse, museum, gift shop and park is one mile farther north at the end of Grand Lake Rd. (CR-405).

OLD PRESQUE ISLE LIGHTHOUSE

NEW PRESQUE ISLE LIGHTHOUSE

96 MIDDLE ISLAND LIGHT

Middle Island, about two miles off-shore halfway between Thunder Bay and Presque Isle Harbor, holds an unusual gathering of abandoned buildings. The structures in the large complex that surrounds the light, though unused for years, still look eerily efficient and capable, as though they are stubbornly but forlornly standing in hope that their residents will return.

A distinctive wide, bright-red band that bisects the white tower gives this still-operating light a splash of color. Small windows open up from various levels inside the conical brick tower, and a row of windows encircles it just beneath the black parapet. A small building joined at the base is too small to have been home to the keepers.

However, one of two huge buildings standing just down the rocky shoreline is actually large enough to have been a dormitory at this former Coast Guard facility. Both its red brick walls and brown-shingled roof are in remarkably good shape, considering it's been abandoned for many years. White trim highlights architectural details around windows and doors, and the gable peaks have also been accented in white. Two porches, at opposite front corners, look out over the turquoise water from beneath arched supports. Nearby, a second building reflects the architectural styling of the first, but on a smaller scale.

Other buildings in the background are more evidence that this place was once filled with the sights and sounds of a bustling compound whose prime focus was on the waters that fill the horizon.

For a unique family adventure, join an excursion aboard the *Island Freighter II*, which takes small parties to Middle Island on weekends between Memorial Day and Labor Day. The boat departs the Rockport Road public access site (between Alpena and Rogers City) twice a day for a three-hour cruise and land tour. For tour information or reservations write to Captain Mike, 9201 Wreck Road, Alpena, MI 49707 or call him at (517) 595-2821.

Members of the Middle Island Lighthouse Keepers Association (5671 Rockport Road, Alpena, MI 49707) are the light's current caretakers.

Three young adventurers about to set off for Middle Island with Captain Mike.

ALPENA LIGHT 97

The Alpena Light stands at the end of a well-worn pier at the mouth of the Thunder Bay River. The small tower consists of an open frame of four steel legs that rise about 40 feet to support the steel lantern above. Painted a bright red, the structure is surrounded by large, protective boulders at the water line and green bushes that brush up against its base. The concrete pier has been reduced to rubble in some places, and small clumps of bushes have anchored themselves between driftwood near the water's edge.

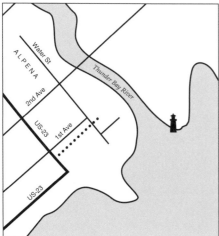

DIRECTIONS: Although this light is not accessible to the public, you can get a good view of it from across the Thunder Bay River. In downtown Alpena one block north of where US-23 makes a 90-degree bend, turn east onto 1st Ave. and go 2 blocks. Park behind either the federal building or the armory and look for the light across the Thunder Bay River, to the right of the rivermouth.

98 THUNDER BAY ISLAND LIGHT

Offshore from the tip of a narrow peninsula near Alpena, the Thunder Bay Island Light, built in 1832, still stands, apparently ready to greet boats searching for Thunder Bay, just around the bend. But the lighthouse and accompanying buildings have been long abandoned, and signs of deterioration abound.

Near the rocky shoreline, the brick tower peers over low-lying bushes to survey the surrounding area. About three stories tall, the once-white tower is capped by a rust-colored lantern and roof. A large, black crack snakes its way down from its tip, and the structure will not stand much longer.

The keeper's cottage, attached to the tower by a narrow hall, is in slightly better shape. Its red-shingled roof is intact and its light-brown brick is punctuated by slashes of white where the windows have been conscientiously boarded up. Nearby, an outbuilding still stands, its red roof and long, narrow smokestack stretching over the jumble of shrubs and small trees that surround it.

As a mute testament to the dangers of the reef that stretches out from the island, the looming shell of a recently wrecked sailboat rests, tipped awkwardly on its side, on the beach about a quarter mile down the shore from the lighthouse. The island is a haven for birds, and they've taken over the hull of the once-proud boat, leaving huge streaks of white across its blue body.

STURGEON POINT LIGHTHOUSE

Five miles north of Harrisville, the Sturgeon Point Lighthouse, whose lamp was first lit in 1870, still stands as a beautiful symbol of our nautical heritage. The Alcona County Historical Society recently saved the brick lighthouse and tower from a dim future of neglect and painted them a crisp white with bright red trim on the window sills and doors. Matching shutters complete the effect, and a reshingling of the roof has brought the building up to date.

The still-active light is owned by the Coast Guard, which opens the 70-foot conical tower a few times each year and

Bill Hanson, a Greenbush resident, is shown holding an award he received from the Sturgeon Point Restoration Group for his services in restoring that lighthouse. Hanson and his family lived at the New Presque Isle, Saginaw Rear Range and Forty Mile Point lighthouses. His Norwegian-born father, William Gustav Hanson, was the First Assistant Keeper at the New Presque Isle Lighthouse and, later, the Saginaw Rear Range Light. Shortly after the end of WWII, the elder Hanson became the keeper at Forty Mile Point.

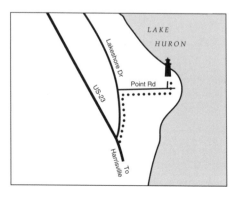

DIRECTIONS: From US-23 about 2.9 miles north of Harrisville, veer right (north) onto Lakeshore Dr. and go about one mile to Point Rd. Turn right (east) onto Point and go about 0.8 miles to a gravel road on the left that enters the parking area. Park near the cable across the road and walk the short distance to the Sturgeon Point Lighthouse, museum and gift shop.

STURGEON POINT LIGHTHOUSE

allows the public to climb its beautiful cast iron stairway. Group tours are also available. Call (517) 724-6297 (summer months only) for further information.

From the top, you see the necessity of having a light in this area. First, there's the shoreline of Sturgeon Point itself, which pulls back on both the north and south sides of the lighthouse. And directly in front of the tower, a strip of gravel cuts through the waves and ends in a finger of sand that quickly dives beneath the water.

The keeper's dwelling, connected to the tower by a brick passageway, is now an excellent museum, with period furnishings that give a glimpse into the past life of the lighthouse. Another building behind the museum holds a gift shop with a nice selection of nautical souvenirs and Michigan memorabilia. The museum is open Memorial Day through Labor Day, Monday through Friday, 10 a.m. to 4 p.m., and Saturday and Sunday from

noon to 4 p.m. From Labor Day through the end of the color season, the museum is open Fridays, 10 a.m. to 4 p.m. and Saturdays and Sundays, noon to 4 p.m.

A lifesaving station, once a part of the complex, was removed, which left an expansive lawn surrounding the lighthouse. The grounds, which are very well kept, stretch beneath several towering hardwoods, and you can site in their shade on a few benches that offer a welcome rest after you've tackled the tower.

TAWAS POINT LIGHTHOUSE 100

Tawas Point, called Ottawa Point until the turn of the 20th century, ranks as one of the most beautiful spots along the Lake Huron shore. The tip of the hook-shaped peninsula is now a state park, and at the park's center stands the lighthouse. First built in 1852 and later rebuilt, it is still in operation and is managed by the U.S. Coast Guard.

The 70-foot-tall conical brick tower sites on a small rise, and its white face is broken only by a small window nearly halfway up the structure. It is topped by a black iron walkway and a 10-sided red roof that matches the shape of the lantern room.

The keeper's dwelling is attached to the tower by a brick passageway. The red-brown brick house, trimmed in white, is large enough to accommodate a lighthouse keeper and his family.

Huge shade trees dot the lawn in front of the complex, and from there you have a beautiful view of Tawas Bay. The state park offers overnight camping as well as day-use facilities. Picnic tables, a pavilion with restrooms and changing rooms, and unequaled sand dunes and beaches make this a beautiful destination.

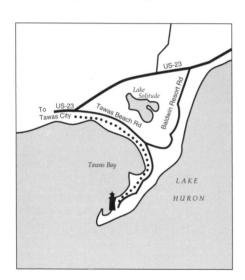

DIRECTIONS: From the junction of M-55 and US-23 in Tawas City, go northeast on US-23 about 1.3 miles to Tawas Beach Rd. Turn right (southeast) onto Tawas Beach Rd. and go approximately 2.8 miles to the Tawas Point State Park entrance. This is a state park fee area.

101 CHARITY ISLAND LIGHTHOUSE

The treacherous limestone shoal surrounding Big Charity Island, which dots the middle of the entrance to inner Saginaw Bay, was first marked by a lighthouse in 1857. But the facility was abandoned in 1939 when the Gravelly Shoal Light began operation, and today the dangerous bottom, which often comes to within a few feet of the surface, is marked with buoys.

In the 1800s the island was home to a prosperous group of fishermen, who used it as a base camp. And investors once considered building a resort here, but were discouraged by the island's lack of a natural harbor and daunted by the prospect of blasting through the limestone shelf under the water to create one.

Unfortunately over the years, the abandoned lighthouse not only became dilapidated but also fell victim to vandals who used the wood siding to build bonfires. Then in late June 2000, a severe wind storm ripped through the area and the large keeper's house was lifted off its foundation, blown over, and completely destroyed.

The circular tower next to it, however, was relatively undamaged, although the elements have left little white paint covering its brick. The black iron lantern at the top is empty, its vacant stare raking across the stone shoreline below.

GRAVELLY SHOAL LIGHT 102

In 1939 the Gravelly Shoal Light and radio beacon was first put into service, and it is still active today. Its round, metal-plated concrete base has an unusual feature: a narrow, curved lip around half its bottom that serves as a dock. A built-in ladder climbs from that near-water-level ledge up to an opening in the chain fence around the top edge of the platform. A small set of stairs leads up into the square base of the white tower, which narrows dramatically above the first level. The corners curve gracefully inward to create the smaller tower, which stretches three more stories above the water. The structure is topped by the narrow finger of a black radio tower, which points upward toward the sky.

103 SAGINAW RIVER REAR RANGE LIGHTHOUSE

The Saginaw River Rear Range Lighthouse, on the west side of the river in Bay City, has been abandoned for many years. But because it is on private property that is difficult to access, the dwelling and tower remain in good condition. The square tower gradually narrows as it rises above the two-story dwelling, and a black iron walkway surrounds the empty lantern room with its painted-over windows. Both the house and tower are constructed of brick painted white, and a wooden addition leans against the rear of the dwelling. An unusual elevated walkway surround both the dwelling and tower about five feet off the ground, and beneath it the house has been expanded in several areas.

You can view this light from the river's shore near the Coast Guard station.

Two groups have joined forces to restore and watch over this lighthouse — the Dow Chemical Company and the Saginaw River Marine Historical Society. Anyone interested in helping with this project can contact the historical society at P.O. Box 2051, Bay City, MI 48707-2051.

104 PORT AUSTIN REEF LIGHT

Port Austin Reef Light — 2½ miles off the tip of Michigan's "Thumb" and visible from shore — first began guiding ships in 1878 and had its own resident keeper until the light was automated in 1953.

Using as its foundation the shallow reef itself, this lighthouse is unusual in several respects. While most shoal lights have square or sometimes round bases, this one is octagonal, which gives it an interesting appeal. In addition, it has its own dock, a narrow concrete extension that juts into the water some 20 feet. The shoal, which comes as close as three feet from the surface, makes it too dangerous for large boats to dock, but skiffs and other small boats once used the platform to bring supplies or visitors from larger boats anchored safely at a distance. The concrete base is streaked with color — black near the waterline and browns and even slashes of white farther up.

The square four-story tower is constructed of chocolate-brown bricks, with four pairs of narrow windows set at regular intervals up its faces. The flat top holds a round parapet and the lantern, which is capped in black metal. Though the light is still in service, its Fresnel lens is gone.

Attached to the tower at its base is a small, square brick building whose red roof can be seen from quite a distance. Inscribed beneath the white peak is "1899," the last year the station underwent major reconstruction. Nearby, a crane stands ready to bring up any needed materials.

This light has recently come under the protection of the Port Austin Reef Light Association (P.O. Box 546, Port Austin,

PORT AUSTIN REEF LIGHT

MI 48467), and they have undertaken the task of restoration and preservation, which is made more formidable by the 2½ miles of water that separates the light from the mainland.

The dangers of the reef here are obvious when you visit the light. Huge rocks loom up from the bottom, and you can clearly see most of the reef through the green waters. Further testament to its many dangers are several area shipwrecks, which have been mapped and set aside as part of the Thumb Area Bottomland Preserve, an underwater park for divers. Offshore caves and huge, old grindstones are among other interesting sights that lie beneath the whitecapped waves.

105 POINTE AUX BARQUES LIGHTHOUSE

Built at the tip of the Thumb in 1848, the Pointe Aux Barques light was the first to guide ships into Saginaw Bay.

The four-story brick tower is perched at the edge of a rocky cliff, which angles sharply down to the waves below, and a light, now automated, still shines from its lantern. Thick trees reach nearly to the top of the white conical tower, and only the black iron walkway, lantern room, and red-domed roof are high enough to look over their tops. The small, white keeper's house is attached to the tower, and an old-fashioned lamp illuminates the front of the brick dwelling when twilight approaches.

The dwelling now houses a museum, but the tower is not open to the public. The beautiful area around the lighthouse is now a county park, with a campground, picnic area with a pavilion, and a wide expanse of shady lawn that stretches to the lakeshore.

The Pointe Aux Barques, which means "point of the boats," complex also originally included a life saving station. During a terrible storm in 1913, crews from this station saved the lives of 33 people when their ship, the *Howard M. Hanna*, was driven off course and went aground off the point.

Today, this life saving station is not only one of the very few that have been preserved, but it also has been moved a few miles west to become a part of a most unusual museum, in Huron City. It is not a typical museum crammed with antiques and mementos. Rather, Huron City has a seven-acre "settlement" of antique homes and buildings, all of which have been realistically furnished with period pieces.

It's easy to spend several enjoyable hours visiting this beautiful, unique town. Not only can you visit the Pointe Aux Barques life saving station, but also an 1837 log cabin, the Huron City church, a well-stocked general store, and a carriage shed, complete with sleighs and other horse-drawn vehicles. A large Victorian mansion is beautifully preserved, and its sweeping expanse of lawn is bordered by a white picket fence. When we visited in June, huge rose bushes were in bloom, and their fragrant flowers burst over the white fence in huge blocks of pink.

The Huron City Museum is open July 1 through Labor Day, 10 a.m. to 5 p.m. daily except Tuesday. Group tours are also available from June 1 through September 30. Call (517) 428-4123 for further information. The museum/gift shop at Pointe Aux Barques Light is open weekends and holidays, 10 a.m. to 6 p.m., Memorial Day through Labor Day or by appointment by calling (989) 428-4749.

DIRECTIONS: From M-25 about 5.7 miles north of Port Hope or 10.2 miles east of Port Austin, turn north onto Lighthouse Rd. and go about 0.8 miles to the entrance to Lighthouse County Park. Turn right (east) and go 0.3 miles to the lighthouse, museum and gift shop.

To get to Huron City from the lighthouse, turn right (west) onto Lighthouse Rd. and go about 2.1 miles to Pioneer Dr. Continue west, on Pioneer, 0.2 miles to Huron City. Look for the visitors center, on your left in the museum complex.

POINTE AUX BARQUES LIGHTHOUSE

106 HARBOR BEACH LIGHT

The Harbor Beach Light, which began shining well more than a century ago, marks the first turn for vessels headed north through Lake Huron. Resting on the tip of a breakwater wall far out from the shore, the light's now-automated lens still guides navigators.

The squat, round tower narrows slightly as it rises four stories above the concrete platform. The brick walls are plated with cast iron, painted white. Four windows at each of the first two levels are trimmed in black and topped by angular black cornices. Several small, black porthole windows also peep out from under the walkway, which is edged by a black iron railing. The round parapet is topped by the 10-sided lantern room, with its rust-colored dome.

Because cut-out areas prevent walking all the way to the light on the breakwater, the only way to get a close-up look is by boat. On land the closest you can get is south of the harbor on the rocky shore in an area that was once the life saving station of Harbor Beach.

Though abandoned for years, the huge buildings have been saved from serious vandalism by being fenced off, and they are still a very impressive sight. A large dormitory stands silent, its vacant watch-tower still peering out from the roof. Nearby, a boathouse stands ready to release wood rescue vessels into the chilly waters below. The boats are long gone, but the feeling of bustling activity still hovers in the air. This compound is a perfect candidate for a refurbishing effort and could easily become a star attraction in the area.

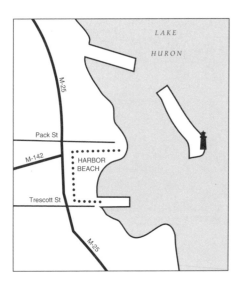

DIRECTIONS: You can get a good view of this light from two areas in Harbor Beach. The first is from the old Coast Guard station. To get to it, from the junction of M-25 and M-142 (State St.), go 4 blocks north to Pack St. Turn right (east) onto Pack and continue (it turns to gravel) to its end.

The other viewing area is 2 blocks south of the M-25/M-142 junction. there, turn east onto Trescott St. and follow it to its end at the beach.

The Harbor Beach Light as it looked in 1935. This photo was printed on a penny postcard that Burt Arkema sent to his wife in Grand Rapids. Arkema was hired to paint the structure and lived in the Harbor Beach area while completing the several-month-long job.

107 PORT SANILAC LIGHTHOUSE

The Port Sanilac Lighthouse is now a private residence, but you can view the picturesque structure from shore and from a pier that stretches out directly in front of it.

The white eight-sided brick tower is interrupted by a lone window about a third of the way up its face. At the top of the three-story structure, instead of the usual bracket-type supports, the brickwork itself flares outward to hold the lantern room and its shiny red roof.

Attached is a charming brick house, with one wall entirely covered in ivy, its green leaves fluttering gently in the breeze. A unique brick facade rises like a set of steps from the center of the dwelling to support a brick chimney.

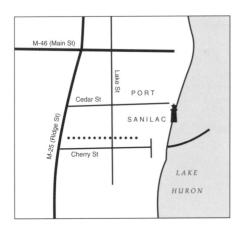

DIRECTIONS: From the junction of M-46 and M-25, in Port Sanilac, go 2 blocks south on M-25 (Ridge St.) to Cherry St. turn left (east) onto Cherry and go 2 blocks to the parking area. You can view the light, which is a private residence, from the parking lot and also from the breakwater that goes out into the lake at the end of Cherry St.

FORT GRATIOT LIGHT 108

The Fort Gratiot Light, on the shore of the St. Clair River near the Bluewater Bridge, was Michigan's first lighthouse. It has stood in some form for more than 165 years and still marks the passage of ships and smaller boats at the entrance to the beautiful yet treacherous river.

Built in 1825, its first keeper would be an appointed federal government official, as were all keepers in the 1800s. As news of its opening spread, a group of influential individuals in Detroit lobbied for their friend George McDougal, a lawyer, to become the keeper. Political pull even-

tually brought McDougal to the shores of the St. Clair River, where the Detroit native's easy life took an uncomfortable turn.

McDougal was appalled by what he found when he arrived. The tower hadn't been built to the government's specifications, and the materials used were so shoddy he felt it was unsafe for him to spend nights in the tower. The keeper's dwelling was no better. The basement often flooded, giving off a foul odor and making it useless as a storage area. There was no root cellar for food storage, and drained his personal savings as he struggled to survive through the winter months. The tower eventually collapsed a few years later, and a much sturdier structure was built in 1829.

Today, the tower, which was rebuilt again in 1861, is still in use as part of a Coast Guard complex and is also protected by the U.S. Coast Guard Auxiliary in Port Huron. Though the area is fenced off, you can still get a good view of the tower and keeper's dwelling from an area on the north side.

Also, the tower is open to the public by appointment only, from May 1 through October 1. To schedule a visit, call Mr. Hanford at (810) 982-3659 and leave your name and number on the answering machine. You can be assured of a call back. You can also phone the staff at the Lightship *Huron*, (810) 982-0891, for further information.

The thick-walled, conical stone tower is white, but the paint has worn away in spots to reveal the red brick beneath. The lantern is covered by a red dome, and a small building is attached to the base of the tower.

Nearby, the red brick keeper's

dwelling and fog-whistle house complete the picture of a stately preserve separated from the bustling city that surrounds it. A bordering fence of heavy white chain divides the lawn from a parking area near the Coast Guard station.

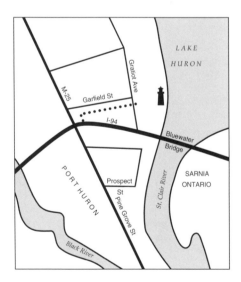

DIRECTIONS: From the intersection of I-94 and M-25 (Pine Grove St.) in Port Huron, go about 6 blocks north on M-25 to Garfield St. Turn right (east) onto Garfield and go to its end at Gratiot Ave. The Coast Guard facility and lighthouse is east of the intersection, and parking is available in the area.

109 LIGHTSHIP *HURON*

Sometimes it was too expensive, difficult or dangerous to build a permanent light near a shoal, reef, or other hazard to navigation. In those cases lightships, equipped with lights atop their masts and foghorns operated by their crews, were often used. They were very arduous and lonely stations. The lightship *Huron*, for instance, was moored on the Corsica Shoals, six miles from the St. Clair River entrance and three miles from the mainland.

The *Huron* retired in 1971 as the last American lightship on the Great Lakes, and today the National Historical Monument is set on the shore of the St. Clair River at Port Huron's Pine Grove Park. "HURON" is still painted in huge, white block letters on the middle half of its nearly 100-foot-long hull. The marking, typical of all lightships, made it easier to identify them when out in the lake. Streamers of multicolored flags, which stretch from the rigging, give the vessel an air of celebration.

You can tour the *Huron* and imagine for yourself what it was like to be stationed for so many months in such a close environment. The *Huron* is open to the public from mid-May through September 2, Wednesday through Sunday, 10 a.m. to 4 p.m. Large groups should

call (810) 982-0891 for an appointment.

Sidewalks line the riverbanks in the park, and there are plenty of benches to sit on and watch the blue water carry its load of ore boats, freighters and pleasure craft.

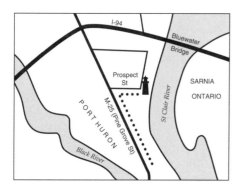

DIRECTIONS: From downtown Port Huron, go north on M-25 (Pine Grove St.) to Prospect St., about ¾ mile south of the Bluewater Bridge. Turn right (east) onto Prospect and go one block to the Pine Grove Park parking areas. The Huron is at the water's edge on the north end of the park. There is a small admission fee to board the ship.

PECHE ISLAND OLD REAR RANGE LIGHT

110

B uilt in 1908 on Peche Island, at the entrance to the Detroit River, this light by the early 1980s was in danger of collapsing. But not only did the Coast Guard replace the aging structure, it also brought the old tower to Marine City, where it is now on display in the Marine City Nautical Park, on the shores of the St. Clair River.

The round, white steel-plated conical tower — its face broken only by a solitary, tiny window — rests near the water, its black, octagonal parapet towering three stories overhead.

A walkway borders a portion of the riverbank there, and benches along the water's edge make it a great spot to relax while watching ships and sails glide up and down the water.

The structure that replaced this tower is near the shore of Peche Island, just upriver from Belle Isle. The tall skeletal tower is topped by a large, red panel with a gray stripe bisecting it from tip to bottom. Atop the panel is a small light. This pattern is reflected in the smaller front range light farther out in the lake.

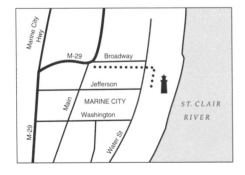

DIRECTIONS: From M-29 at the traffic signal in Marine City, go east on Broadway St. (if you come from the south on M-29, at the traffic signal you are already on Broadway) and go 2 blocks to S. Water St. Turn right (south) onto Water and go 2 blocks.

111 ST. CLAIR FLATS OLD RANGE LIGHTS

You can see the St. Clair Flats Range lights, which are no longer in use, from the shores of the lake at Mt. Clemens or Harsens Island. Although in a serious state of disrepair, both lights are still charming in their own way. It is refreshing to be able to see the old-fashioned brick towers far out from shore before they eventually either crumble beneath the waves or are removed to make way for impersonal, modern steel structures.

The Front Range is a small, round tower of honey-colored brick. Its lantern has been stripped, leaving only a few guard rail posts pointing upward, and a gaping window reveals the blackness within the tower. The light is no longer structurally sound, and the tower leans noticeably. Posted signs warn visitors to stay off the structures.

About a block and a half behind it and closer inland is the Rear Range Light, a two-story tower that, like its companion, shows all the common signs of neglect. The large, white foundation stones have crumbled in places, leaving jagged corners and unfilled holes. The conical tower is made of multicolored brown brick, and two empty windows still look out onto the blue waters below. Portions of the iron lantern room remain, but the inside is bare. The tower is capped by an iron dome that has been whitewashed with the tell-tale sign of birds, who seem to have found the quiet place much to their liking. The keeper's dwelling, once attached, has been removed.

The S.O.S. Channel Lights Association (P.O. Box 46531, Mt. Clemens, MI 48046-6531; (313) 772-1888) plans to completely restore these old structures as funds permit.

LAKE ST. CLAIR LIGHT 112

The Lake St. Clair Light, three miles offshore from the St. Clair Shores area, still illuminates the passage down the lake for the many ships that pass by. The circular foundation platform is plated with iron, and ladders have been built into its wall to provide access for maintenance crews. Atop the platform is the tower's wide octagonal base, its white paint chipped off in large areas. The 30-foot tower itself is much narrower, and half of its eight sides have vertical rows of porthole windows. Its top is bordered by a guardrail that shelters the green light. A green stripe, which was added in recent years, bisects the narrow tower and give it a distinctive appearance.

113 WINDMILL POINT LIGHT

Windmill Point Light stands at the edge of the Detroit River in Mariners Park in the city of Detroit. Rows of rivets highlight the panels used to create the white, conical steel tower. A black iron fence and lantern top the structure, which rests on an octagonal concrete foundation.

A fence that runs from the tower up the shore of the river the length of the park is often used by anglers, who line the railing to try their luck in the deep-blue waters below.

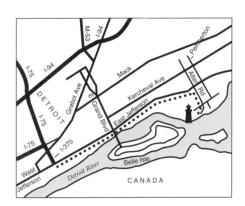

DIRECTIONS: From the junction of I-375 and Jefferson Ave. in downtown Detroit, drive approximately 6.3 miles east on Jefferson to Alter Rd., at the Grosse Pointe Park/Detroit boundary. Turn right (south) onto Alter and follow it a little more than a mile. Near its end, Alter turns to the right (west) and crosses a bridge. As soon as you have crossed over the bridge, look for Detroit Mariner Park and parking area on your left. The Detroit River is less than a block away and the Windmill Point Light is at the south edge of the park.

Although it is not difficult to get to this light, if you are unfamiliar with the area, we recommend that you take along a detailed city map.

WILLIAM LIVINGSTONE MEMORIAL LIGHT 114

The city of Detroit is renowned for many things, but one of its most-individual contributions to the Great Lakes shipping industry — the William Livingstone Memorial Light — lies nearly forgotten on the nation's largest city-owned island park, Belle Isle. The light is unique in two ways. It is the only light in the nation constructed of marble, and it is one of only two lights in Michigan erected as memorials.

William Livingstone, a prominent and popular resident of Detroit, was president of the Lake Carriers Association from 1902-1925. A plaque attached to the side of the tower explains the gift as coming not only from the Lake Carriers Association, but also from the citizens of Detroit.

The tower is a 65-foot-tall fluted marble column with beautiful classical lines. The whiteness of the marble has been dulled by the passage of time, and the once-glistening dome that caps the lantern is now green with age. The tower sits on a wide, octagonal marble foundation, and the heavy metal door that opens to the inside is worked with intricate designs. Unfortunately, not all visitors have treated this historical structure with care. Some have left graffiti on the steps and initials scratched on the metal door.

However, recently volunteers from a local Girl Scout troop cleaned the base of the structure and the steps and also beautified the grounds with a border of flowers. And on our last visit, in 1993, the tower had been recaulked and the grounds well-maintained.

A decorative cast iron fence surrounds the area of the tower, and from this corner of the island, with its stretches of grass and shade trees bending over the water, you can gaze across the river to the contrasting Windsor skyline.

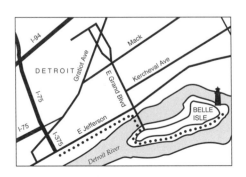

DIRECTIONS: From the junction of I-375 and Jefferson Ave. in downtown Detroit, drive approximately 2.5 miles east on Jefferson to E. Grand River Blvd. Turn right (south) and cross MacArthur Bridge to Belle Isle.

On the island follow the perimeter road to the right, then around the island. As you approach the east end of the island look for the Dossin Great Lakes Museum and then the U.S. Coast Guard station. A short distance after you pass the Coast Guard facility, the road turns to the left. Park in that area and walk along the asphalt paths to the lighthouse, about 1/4 mile away at the tip of the island.

Although it is not difficult to get to this light, if you are unfamiliar with the area, we recommend that you take along a detailed city map.

115 GROSSE ILE LIGHT

The Grosse Ile North Channel Front Range stands at the end of a short wood pier that juts out into the Detroit River on the northeast side of the island. The small cement foundation has been worn away near the water line, and the roof is green with age, but the octagonal, white tower is beautiful. Each face is sided with horizontal wood strips, like on an old house, and near its middle the structure angles inward and narrows. Just beneath the walkway, a miniature window peeps out to survey the blue current below. The eight-sided lantern room is empty and no longer illuminates the darkness of the river.

The structure has been saved by the Grosse Ile Historical Society, which usually sponsors one public tour of the light each fall. For further information, in early summer write to the Grosse Ile Historical Society, East River Road Parkway, P.O. Box 131, Grosse Ile, MI 48138.

DETROIT RIVER LIGHT 116

W here the sparkling expanse of Lake Erie narrows toward its western border, the Detroit River Light welcomes travelers moving up the Great Lakes system. The light has assisted ships entering and exiting the congested and sometimes dangerous area since 1885.

On the six-sided, elongated stone and cement foundation, there is just enough room for the short tower and attached building. The stones have been chipped away in places and their rugged appearance gives proof of the power of waves and ice. The three-story steel-sided tower is wide at the base and narrows only slightly to the top, which gives it a squat appearance. The upper half, including the walkway and lantern room, are painted black, and the lower half is white. The one-story functional building is also white with a dull-red roof, and its metal siding is not broken by the presence of any windows.

The Traveler's Log

Lighthouse visited	Notes
	Date: | | |
	Date: | | |
	Date: | | |
	Date: | | |
	Date: | | |
	Date: | | |
	Date: | | |
	Date: | | |
	Date: | | |
	Date: | | |
	Date: | | |

Lighthouse visited	Notes
	Date: | | |
	Date: | | |
	Date: | | |
	Date: | | |
	Date: | | |
	Date: | | |
	Date: | | |
	Date: | | |
	Date: | | |
	Date: | | |
	Date: | | |
	Date: | | |

Alphabetical Listing of Lighthouses

LIGHTHOUSES YOU CAN ENTER

LIGHTHOUSES WHOSE TOWERS YOU CAN CLIMB

LIGHTHOUSES THAT ARE STILL ACTIVE

LIGHTHOUSES WITH MUSEUMS

CHARTERS

Offshore lights would have been difficult for us to visit. But we contacted charter boat captains in the areas we were interested in, and they were eager to help. Almost all of the boats we chartered were members of the Michigan Charter Boat Association, a group we highly recommend. Every charter we took went off without a hitch, although in some cases the trips were cancelled because of the quickly changing weather conditions on the Great Lakes.

Talk to your captain as you book your charter to find out how many lights you can visit in the allotted time, and also ask for ideas for other places to visit in the area. Almost all of the boats we used were fishing boats, and in some waters you could combine two favorite pasttimes — fishing and visiting lighthouses.

When you go out on a boat, it's a good idea to bring along soft-soled shoes, sunglasses, a hat or cap, sunscreen lotion, rain slicker and jacket. And dress as though it is 25 degrees colder out on the lake because, especially during spring and fall, it probably will be.

We have used the following charters and can recommend them. For a more complete list, write the Travel Bureau, Michigan Department of Commerce, P.O. Box 30226, Lansing, MI 48909, and ask for a copy of *Michigan Fishing and Specialty Charters*.

Alpena Area

Captain Mike Joyce
Black River
(517) 471-2898

Beaver Island Area

Captain Terry Van Arkel
Beaver Island
(616) 448-2407

Detroit River, Lake Erie and Lake St. Clair

Brays Charter Service
Captain Tom Bray
Detroit
(313) 273-9183

Escanaba Area

Take Five Charter Fishing
Captain Dick Stafford
Gladstone
(906) 789-0110

Marquette Area

Catch-a-Finn Charters
Captain John Maki
Marquette
(906) 225-6953

Munising Area

Big K Scuba
Captain Bob Kurth
Munising
(906) 387-2927

Saginaw Bay Area

Alma-D-Charter Service
Captain Dave Harbin
Caseville
(517) 856-4749

Straits of Mackinac Area

Captain Jim Bishop
St. Ignace
(906) 643-9401

Marine Delivery Service
Captain Edward C. Engle
Cheboygan
(616) 617-2025

In some instances, we chose to use aircraft instead of boats. Here we also recommend the following charter services.

South Fox Island, Old Mission and Little Traverse lights

Harbour Air
Cherry Capital Airport
Traverse City
(616) 929-1126

Beaver Island

Island Airways
Beaver Island and Charlevoix
(616) 547-2141

GreenBay/Northern Lake Michigan Area

Peninsula Air, Inc.
2900 Airport
Escanaba
1-800-245-0888

Whitefish Bay and St. Marys River areas

Twin City Air
621 Bingham Avenue
Sault Ste. Marie, MI 49783

THE AUTHORS

The Penrose family resides in rural West Branch, Michigan. Bill, Sr., and Ruth have recently retired from long-time careers and now enjoy spending much more time exploring and photographing the Great Lakes area together. Their daughter Laurie, a high school English teacher, and her husband Ross Rose are the devoted parents of two school-age children, Masina and Alex. Bill Penrose, Jr., is hard at work transforming the thousands of Great Lakes area outdoor photographs the Penroses have taken over the years into a viable family business.

The family is in the process of opening a home-based nautical gift shop specializing in their original framed and matted photographs of Great Lakes lighthouses. The Penroses' photographs are also available at select galleries and gift shops throughout the Great Lakes area. (For the gallery nearest you, call the Penroses at 517-345-3279.)

The Penroses have three other family-effort books to their credit: *A Guide to 199 Michigan Waterfalls*, *A Traveler's Guide to 100 Eastern Great Lakes Lighthouses*, and *A Traveler's Guide to 116 Western Great Lakes Lighthouses*.